Dirk Nowitzki: The Inspiring Story of One of Basketball's Best European Stars

An Unauthorized Biography

By: Clayton Geoffreys

Table of Contents

Foreword

Easily one of the most influential international players to ever play the game, Dirk Nowitzki ushered in a new era of faith in international players making the jump to the NBA. There are few players in the last few decades that have played their entire careers with a single franchise, and Dirk Nowitzki is one of those players. It's with good reason. Dirk is one of the most lethal power forwards to have ever played the game. A legitimate seven-footer, Nowitzki towered over his opponents and dominated both inside and outside. An NBA Champion, it should come to no surprise that when the time comes, Dirk Nowitzki will be a first ballot Hall of Famer. This updated edition incorporates Dirk's later years in the league as a mentor to the new star of the Mavericks, Luka Dončić. Thank you for purchasing *Dirk Nowitzki: The Inspiring Story of One of Basketball's Best European Stars*. In this unauthorized biography, we will learn Dirk Nowitzki's incredible life story and impact on the game of basketball. Hope you enjoy and if you do, please do not forget to leave a review!

Also, check out my website at claytongeoffreys.com to join my exclusive list where I let you know about my latest books. To thank you for your purchase, you can go to my site to download a free copy of *33 Life Lessons: Success Principles, Career Advice & Habits of Successful People*. In the book, you'll learn from some of the greatest thought leaders of different industries on what it takes to become successful and how to live a great life. I'll also gift you a few more of my basketball biographies.

Cheers,

Clayton Geoffreys

Visit me at www.claytongeoffreys.com

Introduction

During the 1980s and 90s, when you saw guys standing seven feet tall hoisting long-range shots from behind the three-point line or shooting turnaround fadeaway jumpers out on the perimeter, you might have been screaming, "Is that guy crazy?!" Head coaches would lose their heads watching the tallest guy on the floor throwing up ill-advised shots. They would rather see them posting up or camping inside the paint. You could even say that big men who were fond of shooting long-range shots often found themselves on the far end of the bench back in the day.

But you cannot blame the coaches. Those big men were products of their time. Back then, the game of basketball had different rules and systems that were designed to enable big men to post up inside the paint and take advantage of mismatches whenever they were near the basket. The game was moderated in a way that allowed guys like Shaquille O'Neal, David Robinson, Hakeem Olajuwon, and Patrick Ewing to dominate the 90s era during what is widely considered the "Golden Age" of NBA big men. Of course, basketball has always been a game of size. And when it comes to size, these seven-footers took advantage of what they had and made it a point to control the game of basketball near the basket.

Fast forward to today's NBA and you will see near-seven-footers such as Kevin Durant playing small forward and making his living out on the perimeter. You will see big men like Kristaps Porzingis, Nikola Jokic, Karl-Anthony Towns, Joel Embiid, and Nikola Vučević camping out 18-to-25 feet away from the basket to shoot jumpers over smaller defenders. And you know what? Everyone is okay with it now.

Nobody goes crazy over seven-footers trying to take over the game with their perimeter shooting anymore. In fact, coaches love it that big men venture out of the paint to stretch defenses and provide open driving lanes for smaller players because those seven-footers are taking paint defenders out of their comfort zones and forcing them to defend the perimeter instead. Because big men are now shooting from beyond the arc, opposing players on defense have to gamble between guarding the three-point line or defending the paint.

Decades ago, nobody thought these types of players could actually impact the game. But now, they are as big a part of the game of basketball as any type of player. So, what changed? Well, there are a lot of factors involved. You can blame how certain players such as Stephen Curry and James Harden made the three-point line more prominent in modern times. You can also look at how Kevin Durant practically made himself a matchup nightmare because he can bring the ball and shoot jumpers despite having the imposing size of a center.

There are so many incremental changes that evolved to allow seven-footers to step out to the perimeter and beyond the three-point line to shoot jumpers. But if you are looking at individual players, there is one special man in particular who has had as much impact as anything else as far as ushering in that change, a big man who came into the NBA in 1998 all the way from Würzburg, Germany and absolutely electrified the league. That man is seven-foot power forward, Dirk Nowitzki.

Nobody knew what to expect from the 20-year-old German kid when he came into the NBA. In 1998, the league was dominated by seven-foot-tall centers like Shaquille O'Neal, David Robinson, Hakeem Olajuwon, and Patrick Ewing, who all made their money by scoring inside the paint. The prevailing attitude then was that seven-footers who took jump shots more than 50% of the time had no business in the NBA, especially not against the prototypical giant center. But then along came a tall and lanky player from Germany named Dirk Nowitzki.

Back in those days, basketball was a growing sport in Europe, and it had a different style of development compared to the United States. In European countries, systems often instill the fundamentals of basketball, no matter the size or athletic abilities of the player. From point guard to center, every player in Europe was trained to pass, dribble, and shoot. That was why legendary European basketball players back in the 1990s such as Toni Kukoc and Arvydas Sabonis were able to do pretty much anything on the court, despite having the size of prototypical big men.

Dirk Nowitzki had all of those skills. Nearly two decades later, he had evolved into an MVP, an NBA champion, a multiple-time All-Star, a member of the All-NBA team more than 10 times, and into one of the greatest NBA players in the history of the game, not just in terms of the standards that are usually set on international players but also in general when you look at how he stacks up against the greatest players the league has ever seen.

The NBA is a "copycat" league. Every up-and-comer wants to be just like the latest and greatest players that dominate their particular eras. And in the 90s, every seven-footer out there wanted to be Dirk Nowitzki. Every team in the NBA wanted a player of his caliber. Every coach wanted their big men to perform like Dirk. They say that you know a player is one of the greatest of all time if he changes the game of basketball to such an extent. Guys like Wilt Chamberlain, Michael Jordan, and Shaquille O'Neal all contributed to numerous rule changes and new basketball tactics that paved the way for today's NBA. Dirk Nowitzki was no different.

Nowitzki made the power forward position into his own by scoring huge numbers with his shooting abilities. With his influence, shooting big men have become a premium because of their ability to stretch the floor and take defenders out of the paint. Teams like the Miami Heat and the Golden State Warriors have won championships with big men that could shoot perimeter jumpers very well. Dirk's incredible and awe-inspiring skill in that capacity truly helped to usher in a new NBA game that gave credence, viability, and importance to that ability.

In a modern NBA that puts a premium on "unicorn-like" stars who are described to be players who have the size of power forwards and centers but the skills of guards, Dirk Nowitzki was the original unicorn. He proved false the notion that seven-footers were not supposed to be shooting jumpers because of how successful he was at doing just that during his prime years in the NBA. You simply could not ignore what he did, both as a star and as a winner who could lead his team to championships on the backbone of those talents. As such, he opened the floodgates for the unicorn movement in the NBA and created an entry point for international players who had the same set of skills.

As an international player, Dirk Nowitzki is arguably the best to ever come from Europe, even compared with great European players such as Pau and Marc Gasol, Tony Parker, and Vlade Divac. And out of all the NBA players who were born outside of the United States, Dirk belongs up there together with the likes of Hakeem Olajuwon and Tim Duncan.

Dirk has been one of the biggest stars of international basketball and has helped the influx of international talent into the NBA with his success on the grandest stage. He is truly an incomparable talent and an icon that has helped make basketball a sensation all over the world. Not only is Dirk Nowitzki one of the biggest stars in basketball, whether in the United States or any other part of the world, but he is also one of the most unique NBA players and a pivotal figure who was able to impact the game of basketball and garner accomplishments in ways most people his size have never done at the same level.

And when Dirk Nowitzki retired from the game, his impact as a player and trailblazer was solidified when teams all over the NBA had seven-footers who could shoot the ball from far distances. Even the Dallas Mavericks made it a point to find a suitable Dirk-like replacement when they made the trade for sweet-shooting 7'3" Latvian big man Kristaps Porzingis right before Nowitzki retired from the sport. That goes to show how much impact this big German has had in the NBA, even during the twilight portion of his NBA career. But talent such as his can never be fully replaced, and we will continue to remember and appreciate Dirk Nowitzki's contributions to basketball for generations to come.

Chapter 1: Childhood and Early Life

Dirk Werner Nowitzki was born to parents Jörg-Werner and Helga on June 19, 1978. Dirk is the couple's second child. He was born in and grew up in Würzburg, West Germany. Würzburg is one of the oldest cities in Germany and was also one of the most devastated places during World War II when it was bombed by the Allies.

Though Würzburg, a city in Germany's Bavaria region, was not a hotbed for athletes and was not really renowned for its ability to develop sports personalities, Dirk was thankful for how his genetics came into play because athleticism ran in the family. Jörg-Werner, in his younger days, was a professional handball player and was considered a world-class, well-known talent in that sport. And his mother Helga was a professional basketball player and spent some time playing for the country's national team. Both of Dirk's parents were also a lot taller than the average person, although neither of them was near the height that Dirk would reach in adulthood.

Dirk Nowitzki's older sister by four years, Silke, also played a lot of basketball in her younger days and was very active in track and field. Silke became a professional baller by the time she turned 20 years old, thus adding more testimony to how athletic the family was. She also benefited from those Nowitzki genetics as she grew up to become six feet tall.[i] As both women in the Nowitzki household played competitive basketball, Jörg-Werner would often tease Dirk that he was playing a women's sport.[ii]

Wanting to follow in his father's footsteps as a competitive handball player, Dirk initially tried playing the sport that made his old man famous. He would later realize that he did not dream of becoming a professional handball player. He also tried to play tennis because he deeply idolized Boris Becker, a former professional tennis player who hails from Germany and who was once the top overall tennis player in the world. However, Dirk was playing taller than most of his peers and most of his contemporaries. As his mother would recall, he stood about a foot higher than most kids his age. Thus, he was often teased for his height, especially when playing tennis.[iii]

His height made Dirk insecure at a very early age. Not only was it hindering him from playing the sport he initially loved, but it also made him the butt of many jokes from other kids. Because of his unusual, early height that never stopped increasing, Helga actually brought him to a doctor to see if there was anything wrong with him. Dirk turned out to be fine, and the doctor predicted that he would be about six feet tall by the time he reached adulthood. That doctor was never so wrong in his entire life.[iv]

What happened next in Dirk's life changed him for the better and was perhaps the best thing to ever happen to him. When he was about 13 years old, his teachers suggested that he play basketball so that he would become more comfortable with his size. Dirk learned to accept and love his growth because every other basketball player he played with and against were also tall players. He began to realize that his height was actually a gift, especially when you factored in how beneficial it is in basketball. Thus, he embraced his height and decided to learn to love the game he would soon play at a superstar level.[v]

Though Dirk would still remain taller than most of his basketball contemporaries, his athletic genetics had him playing at a quicker pace and with more coordination than kids of his size. However, his size would still hinder him in a few ways even in basketball, at least in the initial part of his life. European countries are recognized in basketball for being able to develop a player's fundamentals, no matter their size or what position they play. But Dirk became an exception to that rule. He was initially taught the skills of a center because of his height. Thus, the Dirk Nowitzki we know now was far from the player he was when he initially played basketball. However, that all changed when he turned 15 and met Holger Geschwindner.

Chapter 2: Training with Holger Geschwindner and Playing Professionally in Germany

In 1994 at age 15, Dirk Nowitzki started playing professionally for the DJK Würzburg X-Rays, a professional basketball team based in Würzburg, Germany who were playing in the Second (division) *Bundesliga*. DJK, which stood for *Deutschen Jugendkraft*, means "German Youth Power." While playing for the team, the big German caught the attention of former professional basketball player and German national team member, Holger Geschwindner. The first thing he wanted to do was train the young Dirk and he immediately asked the Nowitzki household if he could mentor their son.

With the permission of Dirk's parents, Geschwindner took the young Nowitzki under his wing. Under his tutelage, Dirk was transformed into a good all-around player, which was something rare for a man of his size. He basically asked Nowitzki if he wanted to be better than a standout star in Germany, or if he wanted to be one of the best to ever play the game all over the world. While "Hotsch," as Dirk called him, would teach the young German the proper shooting form and the basics needed of a fundamentally sound basketball player, his methods were a bit unorthodox. Hotsch had a friend named Ernie play a saxophone while he was training Dirk. He told Dirk to time his movements to the tune of the sax. It might have been a little weird as a training method, but it provided Nowitzki the grace he needed on the basketball court.[vi]

Aside from having Dirk train to the tune of a musical instrument, Geschwindner also had his pupil learn and read different things. He told Dirk that basketball was not everything in life, and he had him read various books on topics that ranged from poetry all the way to physics. Additionally, he was advised by Geschwindner to stay in school, even though he already wanted to drop out of Röntgen-Gymnasium, the high school he attended while playing for the X-Rays. On top of that, Dirk learned how to play different musical instruments. He was truly an all-around man under the tutelage of Geschwindner. How all those things helped him in his basketball career is something we might not ever fully comprehend. All we know for sure is that the mentor wanted to teach his pupil that basketball would eventually end and that there was a lot more to life after a good career with the sport.[vii]

After honing his skills with his mentor and reaching the mature age of 17, Dirk Nowitzki was promoted to the DJK Würzburg's senior team. Though he was already a refined young player, he was often relegated to playing garbage time off the deepest end of the bench as he struggled to adjust with the senior team as well as with his grades in school.

He would become a full-time starter in his second year with the team. Dirk also became a consistent double-digit scorer that season, though he had yet to become the star of the team. At nearly 18 years old, Nowitzki had already impressed German national team head coach Dirk Bauermann enough that the elder Dirk went on to claim that Nowitzki was the best young German talent in the last decade.[viii] After that season, he was offered a spot by FC Barcelona to play in Spain, but he declined because he still wanted to finish his *Abitur*, a designation used in Germany for students who finished their final exams.

In 1996-97, Dirk Nowitzki's third season with DJK, he became the best player and top scorer of the team after Geschwindner took over the coaching reins. He averaged 19.4 points and 9.9 rebounds that year while leading his team to second place. However, ranking second was not good enough to get promoted to the First Bundesliga. In the same year, he also participated in a promotional game held by Nike against NBA players that included Charles Barkley. Nowitzki dunked on Barkley during that game and impressed those who were able to watch. The

NBA superstar commended the young German teenager and even said that Dirk should approach him if he wanted to go to the NBA.

After the season ended, Dirk had to undergo compulsory military service, which lasted for about 10 months. Though he dreaded undergoing almost a year and a half of military service and training, those months strengthened his body and instilled a lot of discipline in the young German kid. However, Dirk was still allowed to play in the Nike Hoop Summit in 1998 during that span of time. He scored 33 points and grabbed 14 rebounds in that game and wowed the crowd with an array of skillful moves that were typically unseen from a man his size. Dirk was ready for the big leagues and he tried his luck in the 1998 NBA Draft. But because of his military service, he was not able to attend any pre-draft camps or training sessions.

After returning from his military service, Dirk Nowitzki already measured more than 6'11" in height. He was also drafted into the NBA via the 1998 Draft. However, Dirk did not yet proceed to play in the United States, as the NBA entered into a lockout period right after he was drafted. In the interim, Nowitzki returned to his team in Würzburg and led them to a first-place finish and promotion. He led the team in scoring with an

17

amazing 28.2 points per game and was chosen as the German Basketballer of the Year in 1998.

Even though he was already drafted into the NBA by the time he finished his fourth season with DJK Würzburg, Nowitzki flirted with the idea of staying in Germany to play for a few more seasons. He even entertained the idea of attending college in the United States to play college basketball. Some of the schools he had his eye on were California State, Stanford, and Kentucky State.[ix] As he said in hindsight, Dirk may have gone on to play for the 1998 Kentucky team that had two future NBA players, Tayshaun Prince and Jamaal Magloire. But instead, Dirk Nowitzki proceeded straight to the NBA as a prep-to-pro player, just like Kevin Garnett and Kobe Bryant.

Chapter 3: NBA Career

Getting Drafted

Because Dirk Nowitzki did not get a chance to work out with teams prior to the 1998 NBA Draft due to his time spent in military service in Germany, not many teams got to see him up close or even got a chance to get to know his brand of basketball. The best glimpse that scouts got from Dirk was his amazing 33-point performance for the International team in the 1998 Nike Hoops Summit. But Dirk did not play against top college prospects or NBA-level talent in that game. It was merely an exhibition game against talented high school players. Thus, as good as he was in that game, he was still an enigma as far as what he could do against the most talented players of his age.

Despite that, there were two coaches who had been keeping their eyes on the young seven-footer out of Würzburg, Germany. The first one was Rick Pitino, who was the head coach of the Boston Celtics back then. Pitino organized a workout for Dirk and was impressed by the German's skillset. Nowitzki had all the tools of a guard for a man his size. He could shoot the ball very well and even pass it like smaller players could. He was so versatile that Pitino compared him to the legendary Celtic, Larry

Bird. Amazed by Nowitzki's abilities, the Celtics head coach was intent on drafting him with the 10th overall pick.[x] He wanted Dirk Nowitzki to become the next Larry Bird with the Celtics and was envisioning a comeback of the glory years of Boston.

The other head coach who was curious about Dirk was the Dallas Mavericks' Don Nelson. While Nelson did not do any scouting as a head coach, he had gotten a good glimpse of Nowitzki in the Nike Hoops Summit and wanted to organize a workout as well. While Dirk was still in the states and on leave from his military service, Donnie Nelson, Don's son, arranged a week-long workout with the German youngster at a local YMCA. It was an ideal workout as they were basically the only ones who got to see Dirk showing off his skills. After seeing him showcasing his abilities, the Nelsons were so impressed that they had no doubts in their minds about drafting him.

Don Nelson knew that the Boston Celtics wanted to draft Dirk with the 10th overall pick in the 1998 NBA Draft. Luckily, the Mavericks had the 6th pick, which meant that they had the chance to steal him away from Boston. Nelson also knew that none of the five teams drafting ahead of them were interested in drafting Dirk because they were all intent on drafting players they were able to see up close in the U.S.-based high schools and colleges. But Nelson had no intention of taking chances; he wanted to make sure he ended up with the player he loved while surrounding him with capable talent.

On draft day, Nelson was an architect of a plan that would ultimately make the Dallas Mavericks one of the best teams in the NBA for years to come. Donnie Nelson was interested in Phoenix Suns point guard Steve Nash, as he had ties with him when the latter was still in college. Don knew that the Suns were interested in Pat Garrity. The Nelsons also knew that the Milwaukee Bucks, who had the 9th and 19th overall picks, wanted to draft Robert Traylor. The problem was, Traylor was seen as a better prospect than Dirk at the time and was sure to be drafted prior to the German.

So, Nelson drafted Traylor with the 6th overall pick instead— and urged the Bucks to draft Dirk with their pick to trade him for Traylor. Also, in exchange for the Robert Traylor deal, the Bucks chose Garrity with their 19th pick and traded him over to the Phoenix Suns. The Suns then shipped Steve Nash to the Mavericks in exchange for the rookie that the Bucks gave them. Mission accomplished.

As complicated as the deal may have sounded, it was a gamble that Don Nelson took in order to get Dirk Nowitzki in Dallas.

He knew that the Celtics really wanted to take Nowitzki and that they may have even traded down just to get him in Boston. But Nelson foiled the Celtics' plans by engineering that master plan of getting Nowitzki while also surrounding him with talented young playmakers.[xi] Though the Boston Celtics were not able to get the player they truly wanted that year, they were still lucky enough to have drafted Paul Pierce, who would soon become their franchise player and a sure Hall-of-Famer.

As aforementioned, Dirk Nowitzki's rookie season had to wait because of the NBA lockout that year and Dirk went back to his Würzburg team in Germany at that time and led them to first place in the Second Bundesliga. Even after playing for DJK Würzburg that year, he still flirted with the idea of staying in Germany or perhaps going to college in the United States. Had he done so, the Dallas Mavericks' maneuverings in order to draft him would have all been for naught. But luckily, Dirk made the right choice by proceeding to the NBA as a Dallas Maverick.

Dirk Nowitzki was persuaded to go to America and join the Dallas Mavericks primarily thanks to the efforts of Don Nelson. Nelson told Dirk that he would allow the young German to go back to his home country twice that year so that he could play for the German national basketball team and help them qualify for the Olympic Games in 2000.[xii] That was a big deal for Nowitzki because he had never stayed outside of his home country for such a long time and because he originally still wanted to play in Germany. However bright his future might have been in the NBA, Dirk would miss his ancient hometown of Würzburg and he would also miss his family, his friends, and his mentor, Holger "Hotsch" Geschwindner.[xiii]

In retrospect, the 1998 NBA Draft class did not have a great depth of talent. Only Antawn Jamison, Vince Carter, Paul Pierce, Dirk Nowitzki, and Rashard Lewis went on to become All-Stars. And if you compare what Nowitzki was able to accomplish in his career to all of the other players drafted that year, it is easy to say that the young German was the best player. He became the steal of the year—not bad for the 9th overall pick who was rumored by some to be less talented than Robert Traylor.

Rookie Season

Dirk Nowitzki came into the league at the most opportune time for a young man who was looking to make an impact in the NBA. At that time, the NBA was looking for a fresh new star who could possibly usher in a new era in the league. Michael Jordan, who had been the face of the league since the 1980s, had just won his sixth and final NBA championship and had just retired after the 1998 Finals. His absence left a gaping hole in the NBA and the league was looking for a crop of young players that they could conceivably take over for Michael Jordan and stir up the same kind of excitement that MJ always did.

While Dirk Nowitzki was someone whom nobody really expected to command the same kind of superstar attention that Jordan had, especially considering that he played an entirely different position and was an unknown at that time, coming into the league in the post-MJ era still allowed Dirk to attract fans and who were looking for a new fresh face to idolize.

But, as mentioned previously, Dirk did not get to immediately play in the NBA after he was drafted, nor was he able to train right away with the Dallas Mavericks before the 1998-99 season got started. Because of labor disputes and certain salary anomalies (particularly Kevin Garnett's), the NBA went into a lockout that did not allow teams to perform basketball-related activities and delayed the start of the season. Because of that, Dirk did not have the time to fully gel with his teammates properly and he struggled to adjust to the NBA's style of basketball in his rookie season, which was shortened to just 50 games.

And thus, Dirk's rookie season did not go as well as he and Nelson planned. The 20-year-old lanky seven-footer struggled to play the power forward position in his first taste of the NBA. Though he was comparatively taller than most of the guys he matched up with, his opponents were faster, stronger, and generally more athletic than he was at the time. He would also only come off the bench as he was adjusting to the NBA. Former NBA champion and veteran ex-Laker A. C. Green started games as the power forward.

Though his rookie year was less than stellar, he did have some bright spots as a first-year player. In only his second game in the NBA, Dirk scored 16 points and grabbed 12 rebounds in a win against the Golden State Warriors. He then followed that game up with a 15-point performance in a losing effort against the Utah Jazz as he was matched up with legendary veteran power forward, Karl Malone.

After those early games, he would find himself playing limited minutes off the bench as the Mavs struggled to win throughout the season. Dirk's best individual performance as a rookie was when he scored a career high of 29 points in a loss against the Phoenix Suns. He shot 10 out 16 in that game and drained two three-pointers. Soon after that 29-point explosion, Dirk began to start most of the games for Dallas as the Mavs were nowhere near playoff contention by that point. He would start the last 11 games for the Mavs and averaged 14 points in that stretch.

Though the Mavs saw what Dirk was capable of given the proper number of minutes, he was still somewhat of a defensive liability. Nowitzki struggled all season long to defend the more athletic power forwards. And if he was tasked to play the center position, he could not contain the bigger and stronger giants in the NBA. As his defense was his main weakness, he was often made fun of and called "Irk" Nowitzki since he had no "D," or *defense,* in his game. The simple truth was, Dirk Nowitzki was still a very young man who had bypassed the more customary transitional college years, and additionally, he was more used to playing offense in Germany, which was vastly different in that it was much less physical. He was yet to adjust to the type of defense he needed to play against the bigger and more athletic players in the NBA.

Nevertheless, Dirk Nowitzki's good performances in his last few games of the season were glimpses of what he was really capable of as a scorer. Moreover, the Mavs had a lot of chemistry emanating from their two new acquisitions, namely Nowitzki and Steve Nash. The two players became quite close as their respective foreign nationalities became a common ground for their friendship. In his rookie season, Dirk Nowitzki averaged 8.2 points and 3.4 rebounds per game while shooting a little over 40% on 20 minutes per game. The Mavericks struggled to win games and limped to the end of the season with a 19-31 win-loss record.

Because of his rookie struggles, and because of how bad the Mavs were performing that season, Dirk briefly contemplated going home to Germany. Back home, he was a dominant offensive force in the Second Bundesliga. He was basically the best player that Germany had to offer. However, Hotsch did not train him just to become the most dominant player *in Germany*. Dirk was trained to become a world-class basketball player who could play and compete with the best players in the world. Knowing that he was better than what his rookie season showed, Dirk Nowitzki stayed in the NBA. And that decision would be a wise one, for he would soon develop to become a force of nature that the league had never seen before.

But in the meantime, what Dirk needed to do at that point was to work on the skills he knew he brought to the NBA, instead of trying too hard to do what all of the other seven-footers in the league were doing. It was his special skills that made him a commodity and a rare kind of player in the NBA. It was important for him to bring something new to the NBA, instead of doing what guys such as Tim Duncan, Shaquille O'Neal, and

David Robinson were capable of doing. He was not a power player or a finesse post-up big man. Instead, he was always a perimeter shooting power forward with the skills of a guard. That should be, and would be, his focus moving forward.

Breakout Season

The events prior to the 1999-2000 season were what really changed the course of the Dallas Mavericks franchise. When Ross Perot, then the owner of the team, admitted that his lack of basketball knowledge was what made the Mavs a sinking ship, he decided to sell the franchise to billionaire Mavericks fan, Mark Cuban. Cuban was a diehard fan of the Mavs and was a season ticketholder. His enthusiasm as a fan carried over to team ownership and he became arguably the most enthusiastic team owner in the NBA, even to this day. Cuban sought to make the Mavs a contender and a more popular team, given that he invested almost $300 million.

Cuban helped the Dallas Mavericks in more ways than they realized. He made it easier for the team to win games by providing the top tools and facilities that his players needed. Even Dirk Nowitzki would go on to say that Cuban was so good at taking care of them that the only thing they needed to focus on was winning.[xiv] One of Cuban's best moves for the Mavs was buying a private Boeing 757 for whenever the team had to travel for games. Cuban also got fans to be more involved and their revenues skyrocketed. Even now, the Mavs are giving away free tickets as a way for them to build their fanbase. That is why the Dallas crowd is as great as it is today. Mark Cuban's dedication helped make the Mavericks a fun franchise to watch but Nowitzki ultimately was the key figure that brought in the fan support.

Because of the change of culture in the Dallas Mavericks franchise, Dirk Nowitzki found it easier to play the NBA's brand of basketball and he was suddenly a full-time starter for the team, even though they had signed legendary rebounding power forward, Dennis Rodman, prior to the season. With Rodman in the mix, Dirk initially started as the center of the team. But Rodman—*The Worm*—would only get to play 12 games for the Mavs that season due to issues off the court. Without their controversial star on the court, Dirk was back to playing power forward, and he played the position so well that he was one of the most improved players in the NBA.

Dirk's minutes and touches increased in his second season in the NBA. He was suddenly finding himself as a focal point for the Dallas Mavericks' offense. Though the scoring load was mostly carried by team captain and veteran Michael Finley,

Dirk was still getting the shots he needed to score some wins for the Mavs. Nowitzki was scoring in double digits throughout his first 20 games for the season, and he only scored less than 10 points twice in that stretch. His best games within those first 20 were both 31-point outputs. The first one was a loss to the Houston Rockets and the second one was also in a losing effort against the Vancouver Grizzlies.

Nowitzki would re-set a new career high in a loss against the Toronto Raptors just 10 games after scoring 31 points for the second time that season. His 32-point performance was his best for the season and in his career at that point in time. Dirk had improved so much as a player that he was named to the All-Star Sophomores team in the All-Star Weekend. In that exhibition game, he played alongside two future Hall-of-Fame players, Paul Pierce and Vince Carter, and then scored 17 points in a losing effort against the Rookie team. Dirk Nowitzki also became the tallest player to become a participant in the All-Star Three-Point Shootout. He would enter the final round only to lose to veteran shooter Jeff Hornacek. Despite the loss, he showed the world that his three-point shooting was not a joke and that it was a deadly weapon given his size and length.

In what became the breakout season for the 21-year-old young man out of Würzburg, he averaged 17.5 points, 6.5 rebounds, and 2.5 assists while improving his shooting to 46%. He played about 36 minutes per game that year, which was almost a 16-minute increase from his rookie season. He was also a runner-up in the Most Improved Player Award voting, just behind Jalen Rose. Together with teammates Michael Finley and Steve Nash, Nowitzki became part of a deadly trio for the Dallas Mavericks for years to come. The Mavs improved their win-loss record to 40-42. Though they did not qualify for the playoffs with their record that season, it was evident that the future of Dallas Mavericks basketball was bright with their seven-foot German leading the way.

First Playoff Season

The Dallas Mavericks kept their core trio of Nowitzki, Nash, and Finley in order to ensure that the team had a fighting chance heading into the new season. They also did not do a lot in the offseason and made only minor additions to the roster, such as adding capable backup guard Howard Eisley and Chinese center Wang Zhizhi, the first-ever player out of China to be drafted into the NBA.

With two years under his belt in the NBA and after learning how to mesh well with his capable star teammates, Nowitzki began to rise as the team's best player and top scorer under the offensive-minded coaching of Don Nelson. Similarly, thanks to Nelson's approach as an offensive strategist, the Dallas Mavericks ended up as a team to watch due to how fast-paced they played the game and how they emphasized a free offense as their go-to game plan. Of course, their offense centered around Nowitzki's ability to generate points in a way that was uncanny for a man standing seven feet tall.

For Dirk's part, he started where he had left off in the previous season. He began the 2000-2001 season as one of the best offensive options the Mavs had in the roster. Dirk duplicated his career high in points in his 19th game of the season by scoring 35 points in a losing effort against the Houston Rockets. He also had a double-double that game by grabbing 12 rebounds.

Five days later, Dirk scored another career high in points. He had 36 points on 13 out of 19 shooting from the field and 5 out 8 from the three-point arc in a blowout victory against the Phoenix Suns. He would continue his scoring rampage in the next 15 games by scoring more than 20 in all but 2 of those games. At that time, Nowitzki was transforming into the Mavericks' best offensive weapon after years of the team relying on Finley for the bulk of the scoring load. His ability to make shots from the perimeter and from all the way out on the three-point line allowed the Mavs to generate offense from the big-man position without having to focus too much on his inside game.

Nowitzki would again establish a new career high in points by scoring 38 points in a win against the Orlando Magic. In that game, he was 12 out of 26 from the field and shot 13 out of 16 from the free-throw line. Not only was he becoming one of the premier perimeter power forward threats in the NBA, but he was also showing the world that he was capable of getting fouls and shooting free throws at a very high rate. He had a season high of 17 rebounds in that game as he further added to his ability as a great all-around player. With Dirk at the helm of the Dallas Mavericks scoring punches, the team became one of the best teams in the NBA as well as one of the most improved.

With Don Nelson coaching the team to a high-octane style and with Steve Nash feeding the likes of Nowitzki and Finley for easy baskets, the Mavs became one of the highest-scoring teams in the NBA and were fourth in most points per game. They were also one of the most exciting groups to watch as they wowed the crowd with a fast-paced style of game that kept people on the edge of their seats, anticipating dunks and three-pointers.

Not fully content with the group they had, however, the Mavs decided to deal for veteran big man Juwan Howard and two other role players in exchange for a package that included former All-Star and original Dream Team member Christian Laettner and several other role players. Howard began starting games for the Mavs at the power forward position and he gave the team the push it needed to finish the season strong. The acquisition of Juwan Howard also allowed Nelson to slide Nowitzki into the center position instead of starting with the slow and offensively-limited Shawn Bradley.

Though the Mavs were one of the most successful teams in the NBA that season and had a trio of excellent players, only Michael Finley, the team's second-leading scorer, was selected to play in the 2001 All-Star Game. Nowitzki and Nash were not selected to the midseason classic, despite boasting star-worthy numbers. Many thought that not including Dirk in the All-Star game was a travesty. But the West was full of equally-good forwards that year and Dirk was just unlucky to find himself behind the likes of Chris Webber, Tim Duncan, Kevin Garnett, Karl Malone, and Rasheed Wallace. It was indeed the age of power forwards at that time, and Dirk Nowitzki was simply playing in a year when fellow power forwards were just as productive and as stellar as he was that season.

Nevertheless, the German power forward ended his third NBA season with 21.8 points, 9.2 rebounds, 2.1 assists, and 1.2

blocks per game. He also improved his field goal percentage to 47.4% as well as his three-point accuracy to 38.7%. Because of his steady performance for the year, Dirk Nowitzki was selected as a member of the All-NBA Third Team despite not making the All-Star squad that season. The 22-year-old also led the Mavs to a 53-29 win-loss record in the regular season and were qualified in the playoffs as the fifth seed.

The Mavericks' first-round opponents were no joke. They were slated to go up against the Utah Jazz, the best Western-Conference team in the mid to late 1990s. The Jazz featured the aging duo of John Stockton and Karl Malone, who were probably the best pick-and-roll tandem in the history of the NBA during their prime years. While both Stockton and Malone were already past their best seasons at that time, they kept themselves in top shape and were ready to face the younger point guard/power forward combination of Steve Nash and Dirk Nowitzki.

In Game 1 held in Utah, the Mavs showed that they were the more inexperienced team as they lost by two points to the more experienced Jazz roster. Then Utah again protected home court by beating the Mavericks in Game 2, 109 to 98. In those two losses, Dirk Nowitzki had a combined scoring number of 35 points.

Dirk came on strong in Game 3. As the series shifted to Dallas, he rallied to the roar of their home crowd. Playing all 48 minutes of the game, Nowitzki scored 33 points as he doubled his output in Game 2 while being just 2 points shy of equaling the points he had in his first two playoff games. He also had a double-double by grabbing 10 rebounds for the Mavericks, who won 94 to 91. The Mavs went on to utterly destroy the Jazz in Game 4. With Dirk making a repeat performance by scoring 33 points, including 5 out of 10 three-point shots, the Mavs handily defeated the Jazz by 30 points to even the series up at two wins apiece.

With only one game left in the opening round, the Mavs returned to Utah to play the Jazz in a close game. While Finley had 33 points to lead the Mavs in that game, and Dirk struggled a bit from the field with his 18 points, it was unheralded role player Calvin Booth who shot the biggest basket of that game as he broke away for an easy layup with less than 10 seconds left. The youth of the Mavs would prevail in that game as they got away with the slimmest of margins over the more experienced Utah Jazz to qualify for the second round of the playoffs.

The second round would not be so easy, however. The Mavs were headed to square off with the top-seeded Western-Conference squad and the team that had the best record in the

NBA. They were set to face the San Antonio Spurs, winners of the 1999 NBA Championship. It was a matchup for the ages as Nowitzki was paired up against the man who would become one of his biggest Western Conference rivals for years to come—Tim Duncan. Both power forwards were among the best young men the NBA had seen in recent years, and both were very good offensive players. While Nowitzki did his damage out on the perimeter, Duncan was a fundamentally sound inside scorer from the post. It was their first playoff matchup, and it would certainly not be their last.

While Tim Duncan was always a good post scorer, he was just as renowned for his defensive prowess. And he displayed that part of his game beautifully by limiting Dirk Nowitzki to only 9 points in Game 1 as the Spurs handily defeated the Mavs by 16 points. Game 2 was no different. Dirk was again playing against a tough defense and was limited to 4 out of 13 shooting for 19 points. He did most of his damage from the free-throw line as the Mavs once again fell to the Spurs in double digits. With Dirk struggling from the field once more, the Mavs lost again by 14 in Game 3.

No team in league history has ever come back from a 0-3 deficit in a seven-game series to win. As insurmountable as their task seemed, Dirk Nowitzki would not allow the Mavericks to go quietly into the night and refused to submit easily to the mighty Spurs. Armed with renewed vigor, Dirk scored 30 points on 11 out 18 shooting to help the Mavs extend the series to at least one more game. However, that one-game extension was all he and his teammates could muster up. Nowitzki would once again play out of his mind in Game 5. But it seemed like he was playing like a one-man team to score a then-career and playoff-high of 42 big points. He also grabbed a career playoff-high of 18 rebounds that night, but it was all for naught because the Mavs lost by 18 points.

Though Nowitzki and the Dallas Mavericks experienced a second-round exit in the best season the franchise has had in more than a decade, they were able to showcase their prowess by beating a more experienced Utah Jazz team in the first round and by refusing to easily submit to the San Antonio Spurs in the Conference Semifinals. Best of all, Dirk's monstrous scoring performances in the playoffs were an indication of what he would deliver for the Mavs in future seasons.

Dirk Nowitzki the All-Star

After the stark improvement to Dirk Nowitzki's game and growing confidence during the 2001-2002 NBA season, and especially after what he showed in the playoffs, the Dallas

Mavericks were beginning to see that their seven-foot German had the makings of a future franchise player. Seeing that they had a chance to build a whole franchise on Dirk's slender shoulders, the Mavericks extended his contract and offered him a whopping six-year, $90-million contract.

Naturally, Nowitzki agreed to the contract and in doing so, he became one of the highest-paid professional athletes to have come from Germany. He was second only to Ferrari's Michael Schumacher in terms of salary. The Mavs kept their core intact that season while also adding veteran guard Tim Hardaway. They would also acquire Nick Van Exel in the middle of the season, and the former Laker point guard served as a capable sixth man for the Mavs.

In the 2001-02 season, Dirk Nowitzki proved that he was the real deal and that he still had a lot of room to grow. He had 8 games of scoring more than 30 points in the first 20 games of the season. In 5 of those games, he had more than 10 rebounds. He was just simply *beasting* for the Mavs on both the scoring and rebounding ends.

Nowitzki went on to score more than 30 in three more games before he would re-establish a new regular-season career-high. He scored 40 points in a win over the Atlanta Hawks as he shot

12 out of 22, including 6 three-pointers, while also grabbing 11 rebounds. After his 40-point game, Dirk scored 32, 34, and 39 in the next three games, which were all wins. He also had 13 rebounds in his 39-point game against the New Jersey Nets.

Dirk slowed down a bit in his next six games until he scored 38 points and grabbed 17 rebounds in an overtime win against the Indiana Pacers. At that point in time, Nowitzki was already a legitimate NBA superstar and there was no stopping him. Not only did he have a great shooting stroke from anywhere within 25 feet of the basket, but he also added a lot of moves down at the low post. His go-to move was always his one-legged turnaround fadeaway jumper that he could shoot over any kind of defense. He was truly a joy to watch on the court because of his unorthodox style of basketball.

Because of the amazing season Dirk was having, he was chosen as an All-Star for the very first time in his career, together with his good buddy and teammate Steve Nash. In the very first of what would be ten All-Star games in his career, Dirk Nowitzki scored 12 points and grabbed 8 rebounds. At the end of the season, he averaged 23.4 points, 9.9 rebounds, 2.4 rebounds, 1.1 steals, and 1 block. His efforts got him into the All-NBA Second Team. He was even mentioned in the MVP conversation and was 8th overall in the voting for the award. His fifteen 30-

10 scoring-rebounding numbers were third only to Shaquille O'Neal and Tim Duncan that season. Best of all, the Dallas Mavericks were rising. The Mavs improved to a 57-25 win-loss record and had emerged as a force to be reckoned with, although they could only get the fourth seed in an ultra-competitive Western Conference.

The Mavericks' first-round opponents were the Minnesota Timberwolves led by Kevin Garnett. It was yet another good matchup of two power forwards who would battle out for supremacy in the position for several more years to come. Nowitzki, as we know, was always a versatile offensive player because of his ability to shoot jumpers at a very accurate pace. Garnett was not so different. KG was also relying on racking up points with his ability to hit perimeter shots. He was also a very good passer and might have even been slightly better than Nowitzki at that time in their respective careers. But his range was not nearly as deadly or as deep as the big German's. Nevertheless, it was still a battle for the ages as the two met in the playoffs for the very first time.

Dirk and the Mavs immediately pounced on the Wolves from the opening bout. Garnett was basically a one-man show in Minnesota and Nowitzki took advantage of that. KG was always a very good defensive player, but he could not cover the whole

Mavericks team by his lonesome. With that, Nowitzki scored 30 big points in Game 1 and grabbed 15 boards as well. He was efficient from the floor and shot 10 out 19 to help the Mavs win 101 to 94. Dirk followed up his Game 1 performance with equally great numbers in Game 2. He scored 31 points and grabbed 15 rebounds yet again, though he would eventually foul out of that game. But there was no need for him to stay longer as he had already done sufficient damage—the Mavs cruised on with a 12-point win to take the commanding 2-0 lead. Nowitzki and the Mavs would not allow the series to extend any longer as Dirk topped his last two performances by scoring 39 points and grabbing 17 rebounds in Game 3. He was simply unstoppable in the whole series as they went on to win the game by 13 points.

In his fourth straight playoff series, Nowitzki matched up yet again with another star power forward: In the second round of the 2002 Playoffs, it was the very talented Chris Webber of the Sacramento Kings. He was one of those power forwards that could basically do everything on the floor, from passing to shooting, posting up, and rebounding. Webber and the Kings were enjoying one of the best seasons in their franchise's history and they were just as good on the offensive end of the floor as the Mavs were, if not better. But the most impressive thing about the Kings was their unselfishness in passing the ball around, and that was what made them the top-seeded team in the West that year.

After an easy first-round matchup, the Mavs were immediately perplexed in Game 1 of the second round. The Kings ran roughshod over them as they cruised on to beat the Mavs 108 to 91. After a historic three-game stretch in the opening round of the playoffs, Nowitzki was limited to 23 points on 8 out of 24 shooting. He did have 14 rebounds, but they were in a losing effort. The Mavs would take revenge, however, by stealing Game 2 on the Kings' home floor. Dirk shot only 15 field goal attempts for his 22 points. He also had 15 boards to help the Mavericks to an 8-point win.

The Kings responded by buckling down for the rest of the series. They immediately took home court advantage back by beating the Mavs on their own home floor. Dirk's 19 points in that game were his lowest in the whole playoffs that season. His 5 boards were also his lowest. He played all 48 minutes in Game 4 and scored 31 points while grabbing 12 rebounds and assisting on 7 baskets. His all-around effort was rendered useless, unfortunately, as Sacramento went on to take a commanding 3-1 lead. Not wanting his season to end in the second round yet again, Nowitzki shot his way to 32 points in Game 5 while also getting 12 boards. But once again, his efforts could not help the Mavs beat the Kings as they fell in the series 1-4.

Dirk's fourth season in the NBA may have ended yet again with a second-round exit from the playoffs, but it was the best season he had had since coming into the NBA. He became an All-Star and ended the season strongly with a Second Team selection because of his efforts in leading the Mavs to a good playoff seeding. And if you thought he had peaked that season, think again. The best was yet to come.

Getting Past the Second Round

Dirk Nowitzki was four years into his NBA career and entering his fifth. In his first four years, he made it into the NBA playoffs only to lose to the top-seeded team in the second round. In his fifth season with the Mavericks, Nowitzki continued to help cultivate a winning culture that would make the Mavs one of the favorites for the NBA title that year.

Keeping their core trio intact together with their best bench scorer, Nick Van Exel, the Mavs raced ahead to one of the best starts in NBA history. The Mavericks were one of the deadliest scoring teams in the NBA but the problem was their defense. In the 2002-03 season, it seemed as if they were putting more effort into their D because they were blowing out a lot of opponents at the start of the season. Dirk and the Mavs went on to a 14-0 start and were merely one victory away from tying the record set by the Houston Rockets in one of their championship seasons in the mid-90s. Their winning streak was finally ended by the Indiana Pacers on November 28, 2002, however. In that 14-0 start, Dirk remained the focal point of the offense, but it was a team effort as he did not have to score more than 30 in all but one of those games. He did have 10 double-doubles in that stretch, though.

Nowitzki remained consistent, though his team would not enjoy the same success that they had at the start of the season. He scored 40 points in a losing effort against the Milwaukee Bucks on December 30, 2002. That was his highest-scoring game that season and was his only 40-point output. His consistency, however, allowed him to have a lot of stretches wherein he scored 30 or more points. While most people thought Dirk was already in his peak the previous season, he demonstrated that he still had the capacity to get even better as his scoring numbers continued to rise.

Because of his efforts that season, Dirk Nowitzki was selected to the NBA All-Star Game for the second time in his career. It was also teammate Steve Nash's second appearance in the midseason classic. Dirk scored 9 points in only 16 minutes of play in that season's All-Star game. And at the end of the season, he averaged 25.1 points, 9.9 rebounds, 3 assists, and 1.4 steals. Those were all career highs at the time.

Dirk Nowitzki was yet again a member of the All-NBA Second Team as he led the Mavs to a historic 60-22 win-loss record, their franchise's best regular-season record. Despite the 60-win season, they were only the third seed in the West, as that conference was as crowded with hot teams as it had ever been, especially when you consider the fact that the San Antonio Spurs, Sacramento Kings, and Los Angeles Lakers were all title contenders as well. Six teams in the West won 50 or more games. Meanwhile, the East only had one 50-win team that year. That goes to show how tough the competition was in Dirk's conference.

For the fifth-straight playoff series, Nowitzki was matched up with an All-Star power forward as they were set to face the Portland Trail Blazers in the first round of the 2003 Playoffs. While former NBA champion Scottie Pippen led the Blazers, much of the scoring and rebounding load fell on Rasheed Wallace. Wallace had as much shooting range as Dirk did, but was not as prolific of a scorer as the German was. Nevertheless, Wallace was known for his never-back-down, tough-as-nails attitude and was one of the most physical players in NBA history.

The Mavs handily defeated the Blazers in the first three games of the first round. Dirk established a new career and playoff high in Game 1 by scoring 46 big points. The Mavs went on to win that game by 10. Game 2 was closer, as the Mavs only won it by four points with Nowitzki scoring 25. Dallas took an insurmountable 3-0 lead by winning Game 3 by 12. Nowitzki had another big night that game and scored 42. The Dallas Mavericks were looking like they were easily headed for another second-round appearance. But it all went downhill from there.

Portland quickly bounced back and won three straight games of their own. Dirk scored 26, 35, and a humiliating 4 points in that three-game losing streak. With the series tied at three wins apiece, it was suddenly now looking like the Mavs would become the first team in NBA history to lose a seven-game series after leading 3-0. But Nowitzki, especially after his awful Game 6 performance, would have none of it. He scored 31 points in Game 7, including a clutch three-pointer in the dying moments of the game to give the Mavs a six-point advantage with 80 seconds left. Dirk would later call that shot the most important basket of his career. The Mavericks won that series by the grace of that shot and took Game 7 107 to 95.

When asked about his performance and his big shot against the Portland Trail Blazers in what was a very critical game, Dirk simply said that he did not want to go home early at that point in his career and that going for a vacation was not an option for him. It was there when the killer instinct of the young German became so apparent, as he had become so competitive to the point that he could ball out whenever his team needed him to do so.

The second round was a rematch against the Sacramento Kings, the very same team that had eliminated them the previous season. But this time, the Mavs were better defensively and their key players were more mature. Still, Dirk struggled for most of their second-round meeting with the Kings. He scored only 18 in an 11-point loss in Game 1. The Mavs bounced back quickly to win Game 2 by 22 points, however. Nowitzki had 24 in that game. Then in a historic, double-overtime thriller in Dallas, Dirk logged in 58 minutes and scored 25 points to help his team win the game by 4.

The two teams alternated wins in the next three games as the Kings went on to tie the series and send it to a deciding Game 7.

Dirk had 11, 16, and 21 respectively in those three games. With emotions running high, he was even ejected in Game 4 after a show of frustration. But Nowitzki would become clutch on both ends of the court in Game 7. He played the toughest defense he had ever played in his five years in the NBA and he even finished the game with 30 points, the highest he had had in the entire series. He also had 19 rebounds in a tough and physical ending to one of the best playoff matchups in recent years.

In the Western Conference Finals, the Mavs would once again face the San Antonio Spurs. Dirk and his team were thinking about revenge since the Spurs had wiped them out of the second round two seasons ago. Once again, it was slated to be an epic matchup between two of the best power forwards the league had to offer. With Dirk losing the last playoff matchup between the two premier power forwards in the NBA, he was looking to get revenge and secure a trip to the NBA Finals for the first time in his career.

With Dirk Nowitzki playing one of his best playoff games, the Dallas Mavericks were able to steal home court advantage away from the Spurs by winning Game 1 113 to 110. Dirk had 38 points on 10 out of 19 shooting as he shot 17 out of 17 from the foul stripe. He also chipped in 15 rebounds that game. The Spurs then regained composure and defeated the Mavs in Game

2 by 13. Nowitzki had a good game that night, but his 23 points and 10 rebounds were not enough to stop the Spurs from tying the series at one win apiece.

Back in Dallas, the Mavericks were looking to win both home games to get a commanding lead over the series, but tragedy struck. As Dirk was going up for a rebound against Spurs guard Manu Ginóbili, he collided knees with the Argentinian star and was forced out of the game by an injury. He only had 15 points that game while playing 40 minutes in a loss to the Spurs. The injury would sideline Nowitzki throughout the entire series. While the Mavs would still go on to win one more game without their leading scorer and best player, they ended up falling to the eventual NBA champions after six games. In hindsight, had Dirk not been injured, the Mavs may have had a good chance of claiming the West title and possibly even the NBA championship trophy against the New Jersey Nets.

Unfortunately, there was nothing Dirk Nowitzki and the Dallas Mavericks could do at that point in time, especially when no one could turn back time and allow the German to avoid getting injured. And even if Nowitzki had not been injured in that matchup with the San Antonio Spurs, there really was no guarantee that the Mavs would have won that series. The best they could do was to be optimistic that their superstar would get back to full form and even improve in the next season so that they could once again have a chance at a Finals berth.

Playing as the Starting Center

After the disappointing injury to Nowitzki in the playoffs, the Mavs' weakness was exposed, as they lacked frontline scoring without him in the lineup. In effect, they were handily defeated by the Spurs in the Western Conference Finals. Intent on adding more scoring on the wing and from the frontline, the Mavs brought in two high-scoring borderline All-Star players in Antawn Jamison and Antoine Walker. Jamison was acquired for a package that included the Mavs' sixth-man guard, Nick Van Exel. For Walker's part, he was brought in in exchange for Dallas' starting center Raef LaFrentz. Without Raef, and with the power forward position in a logjam, Dirk was forced to play as the starting center, a position he was never particularly comfortable with since he came into the NBA.

But the Mavs had no choice because no other player in the lineup, other than the 7'6" injury-prone Shawn Bradley, could play the spot. With that in mind, Walker started as the power forward and Jamison came in off the bench as the replacement sixth man. The Mavericks also acquired rookies Josh Howard and Marquis Daniels in that season's draft. The two rookies became immediate impact players for the team because they were comfortable with the high-scoring style of the Mavs.

With their power forwards and starting center shooting well from the outside primarily as jump shooters and thanks to the added firepower that Jamison, Walker, and Howard provided, the Mavericks were the highest-scoring team that season and had one of the best offensive ratings at that point in the history of the league. The Mavs' fast-paced style favored their scorers and they once again found themselves heavy favorites for one of the top playoff spots in the West.

Historically, Dirk Nowitzki was never comfortable playing the center position. He was a mismatch on offense while playing that role because he brought opposing big men out of the paint. He was also more agile than most of the NBA's big centers in those days. However, Dirk was a defensive liability while playing the center spot. As tall and lanky as he was, he was never a very good shot blocker and never as big or as strong as most other NBA centers back then.

In an effort to remedy his weaknesses, Dirk Nowitzki basically lived in the weight room in the offseason and bulked up by as much as 20 pounds of muscle while sacrificing a bit of his quickness. The added bulk gave Dirk a lot of lower body strength that allowed him to stand his ground against opposing centers. It also allowed him to play from the post more; he eventually developed as a fantastic post-scorer with his back-to-the-basket and face-up games.

Though Nowitzki would get his usual high-scoring numbers of more than 20 or 30 points night in and night out, he struggled with consistency. There were more than a handful of games where the struggle of defending bigger and stronger men took its toll on him. He would score less than 10 points in several of those games as well as being saddled with a lot of fouls. There were also games where he could not gel well with the team's new acquisitions and, in effect, the Mavs would lose handily every time. However, Dirk would still get a few bright spots in the season. He scored a career regular-season high of 43 points in a win against the Seattle Supersonics. He also poured in eight three-pointers that game and could not miss from beyond the arc. Five games later, Dirk would yet again score crazily as he poured in 40 points to help the Mavs win against the Detroit Pistons.

Nowitzki's efforts as the Dallas Mavericks' leading scorer and rebounder earned him another ticket to the NBA All-Star game. He contributed a scant two points in the midseason classic. However, his teammate Steve Nash would not be selected as an

All-Star after two years of being one of the best point guards in the league. Another unfortunate thing was that the Mavs did not play as well as they did in the previous season, though they were still one of the best teams in the NBA because of their explosive offense. They still made it into the playoffs with a 52-30 win-loss record and earned the fifth seed in the West. At the end of the regular season, Dirk Nowitzki's scoring and rebounding numbers decreased after five straight seasons of gradual increases. He averaged 21.8 points and 8.7 rebounds. His defensive stats, however, would benefit from his offseason work, averaging 1.2 steals and 1.4 blocks that season while earning a spot in the All-NBA Third Team.

The Mavs met the Sacramento Kings in the playoffs for the third straight season. With the Kings having home court advantage, luck and favor were not on the side of the Mavs. Nowitzki would play a splendid Game 1, but the Mavs could not stop the Kings from winning the game by 11. Dirk had 32 points and 13 boards that night. Game 2 was played a little bit closer, as the eventual winner merely got away with a four-point win. Dirk had 28 points and 10 rebounds that game, but the Mavs still fell short of stealing home court away from the Kings.

The Mavericks would find their groove back home in Dallas for Game 3. This time, there was no need for Dirk to score huge numbers as he ended the game with 21 points to go along with 8 rebounds. The Mavs easily defeated the Kings 104 to 79. But that was all she wrote for the Mavs. The Kings beat them by two points the following game and sent the Mavericks to an elimination game. In Game 5, Nowitzki poured in 31 points and 14 rebounds, but he could not help the Mavs beat the Kings, who won the game by the slimmest of margins. The Mavs were sent packing in the first round for the first time since acquiring Dirk and after almost reaching the NBA Finals the previous season. It was a disappointing season for the Mavs and one that would change the franchise's fortunes just a few months later.

Without Steve Nash, A New Look for the Mavs

A lot of changes happened on the part of the Mavs both before and during the 2004-05 NBA season. One of the most glaring changes was the departure of Steve Nash from Dallas. The then 30-year-old starting point guard was not an All-Star the previous season and the Mavs front office were not willing to give him a lot of money because of the salaries they were already paying to Dirk and the other All-Star acquisitions the previous season. The most that Cuban was willing to give the two-time All-Star playmaker was about $9 million per year for four seasons.

While Nash was not really expected to command a maximum contract at that point in his career, $9 million a year was too little an amount for his standards and he went on to accept a six-year, $63-million offer made by the Phoenix Suns, his former team. Without Nash, the Mavs were without their best playmaker and the man who fueled their high-octane offense. Steve Nash went on to win two MVP awards in his first and second seasons back with the Suns. For Cuban's part, he was disappointed at how Nash had not been able to give them the same production he gave to Phoenix.

The Big Three era in Dallas was over when Nash left for the Suns. Meanwhile, Finley was getting older and slower and could no longer play at the All-Star level he once played at. So, the Dallas Mavericks went on to build around Dirk Nowitzki as their unquestioned franchise superstar. He was now the lone star in Dallas and had to carry a heavier load without Nash in the mix and with an aging Finley.

The team was forced to retool and rely on other players to fill in the gap that Steve Nash left. The Mavs made moves that brought in center Erick Dampier to man the middle and to move Dirk back to the power forward position where he was at his most effective. They also traded for wingman Jerry Stackhouse, who was traded together with rookie point guard Devin Harris in exchange for Jamison. Lastly, one of their best moves of that offseason was the acquisition of offensive guard Jason Terry from the Atlanta Hawks. With four new key players joining the team together with another new acquisition, Keith Van Horn, the Dallas Mavericks looked like a team far different from the roster they had just a few months previously. And what they did not know yet was this version of the Mavs team was better than when they had Steve Nash.

Even without his best friend and playmaker Steve Nash, Dirk Nowitzki was still able to perform at a high level, if not his highest level since his rookie season. He immediately poured in 33 points in a win against the Kings in their opening game. He scored in high double figures in the next four games and then exploded in three straight games. Dirk first scored 41 in a blowout win in Miami. Two nights later, he would get 31 points in another blowout win against the Nets. The following day, Dirk scored 32 points in a 9-point victory against the Washington Wizards. If you already thought that Dirk was impressive in that stretch of games, the big German would have a career-high 53 points against the Houston Rockets on December 2, 2004. He shot 21 out of 22 free throws in that game and also chipped in with 16 rebounds.

Nowitzki was spectacular that season as the floor was wider due to the availability of more scoring options on the part of the Mavericks. From his 21st game up his 40th of the season, Nowitzki scored more than 20 points in all but two of those games. Though they did not have a prolific playmaker on the team, the Mavericks had a more balanced roster because they had a lot of scoring options in the likes of Finley, Terry, Stackhouse, and the much-improved sophomore, Josh Howard. Basically, everyone on the team was contributing on the offensive end and their defense was not too shabby either as Dampier's size made him more than capable of defending in the paint.

Because of the continued success the Mavericks were seeing despite a totally new look on their part, and because of Dirk's amazing season that year, the big German was once again selected as an All-Star and contributed with 10 points, 4 steals, and 4 blocks in that game. However, the Mavs longtime leader Don Nelson stepped down as head coach by the tail end of the season and chose to resume the duties as general manager of the franchise. He named assistant coach Avery Johnson as his replacement. The Mavs were 42-22 with Nelson and 16-2 with Johnson.

The Mavs ended with a 58-24 win-loss record and were fourth in the Western Conference thanks to the new acquisitions and Dirk Nowitzki, who was playing at an MVP level. Their franchise player had the best season of his career at that point as he averaged 26.1 points, 8.7 rebounds, 2.7 assists, 1.2 steals, and 1.4 blocks. Amazingly, he never scored below double digits that season and his lowest point output was 11. Nowitzki made the All-NBA First Team for the first time in his career, becoming the first player in NBA history to be named to the NBA's best five players without having gone to an American school. Dirk finished third in MVP voting behind former teammate Steve Nash, who had energized the Phoenix Suns that season, and behind Miami's dominant center, Shaquille O'Neal.

In the first round of the playoffs, Dirk and the Mavs would face a team with a little international flavor of their own. The Houston Rockets had 7'6" Chinese center Yao Ming, who had become the most popular international player in the entire world thanks to the sheer population of China, manning the paint and intimidating opponents with his combination of size, skill, and mobility. If the gigantic man in the middle was not scary enough, the Rockets also had two-time scoring champion Tracy McGrady dwelling out on the perimeter.

The Rockets would immediately take the fight to their higher-seeded opponents and stole home court advantage with a 12-point win. Dirk had 21 points that game but was outplayed by McGrady's 24. The Mavs lost both of their opening home games as Yao dominated with his 33 points. Dirk had 26 points that game. But Dallas would take revenge in Houston by beating the Rockets on their own floor in Game 3. Nowitzki had 28 points that game. Although Dirk struggled to get only 18 points in Game 4, the Mavs would take back home court by beating the Rockets twice in Houston thanks to the 32 points scored by Jason Terry.

The Mavericks would finally get a game in Dallas thanks to a 3-point win in the American Airlines Center. Dirk had a double-double with 23 points and 13 boards. But the Rockets would also win a home game by beating the Mavs back in Houston in Game 6. It was a blowout 18-point win, mostly thanks to the 37 big points of T-Mac. Nowitzki struggled again with 14 points, his lowest in the postseason that year. However, Dallas would not fold and they gave their toughest fight to Houston in Game 7. It was an all-around game as Nowitzki rallied back with 28 points and Terry had 31 for a blowout 40-point win on their own floor.

In the second round, the Mavs would see a familiar face, someone who played the best possible basketball on another team—Steve Nash. Nash was the MVP of the season after not even being an All-Star with the Mavs the previous year. He rejuvenated a struggling Suns franchise and took them all the way to the best record in the West. In that series against the Mavs, Dirk's best friend had something to prove to the Dallas organization—that he was worth more than the paltry $9 million a year they had offered him before his departure to the Suns.

In Game 1 played in Phoenix, Dirk Nowitzki filled the stat sheet with 28 points, 13 rebounds, and 4 assists. But his team could not stop the explosive scoring of the Suns. Amar'e Stoudemire had 40 points and Nash had 13 assists in a blowout 25-point win over Dallas. In Game 2, the Mavs played better defense and prevented the Suns from running roughshod over them. They stole a home game in a two-point win. Dirk had a double-double with 23 and 12. The Suns, however, took back home court advantage by blowing out the Mavs again in Dallas. Dirk had 21 and 13 in that game, but Stoudemire exploded for 37 points, helped by 17 assists from Nash.

Steve Nash then exploded for 48 points in Game 4. But it was in a useless effort because Nowitzki, who scored just above half of what Nash had, powered the Mavs to tie the series at two games apiece. Nowitzki and Nash would battle each other out and both scored 34 in Game 5. But Nash's team came out as the victors. With the Mavs reeling and finding themselves on the cusp of elimination, the Dallas-based organization forced overtime in Game 6. But again, it was Steve Nash, the man Cuban let go in free agency, who torched the Mavs for 39 points as he outscored his good buddy and former teammate Nowitzki for virtually the whole series. It was yet again a disappointing playoffs for Dirk Nowitzki and the new revamped Mavericks team.

Breaking Through to the Finals

Prior to the 2005-06 season, the Mavericks completely got rid of any remnants of their Big Three era by waiving Michael Finley's contract. Finley used to be their best scorer and was second to Dirk in that regard when the latter improved to become a franchise superstar. However, age and the wear and tear of the NBA game got to Finley, and he was no longer the dependable scorer he once was. The Mavs would sign the likes of defensive specialists Doug Christie and DeSagana Diop in order to improve the capabilities of the Mavs on that end of the court.

Meanwhile, on offense, Dirk Nowitzki was still their top option but the Mavericks began to lean more on other offensive players such as the quick-firing Jason Terry and the improving future All-Star, Josh Howard. It was by having the offense centered around him that Nowitzki was truly able to rise as an MVP contender while leading the Dallas Mavericks to one of the most successful seasons the franchise had ever seen.

Dirk would once again have a terrific season, despite leading a new core of players. He would not score under 10 points the whole season and his early season low was a respectable 14 points. Though Dirk would not have explosive scoring games above 40 points (his season high was 38), he did improve his consistency as he would reliably score in the high 20s to 30s. This was mostly thanks to his improved field goal scoring and to the improvements of teammates, who helped alleviate the defensive pressure off him. And instead of relying so much on his outside shot, Nowitzki began to explore the post more often and utilized his ability to take defenders out of the paint with his face-up jumpers and midrange shots.

But Dirk was not the only player on the team who was succeeding in that season. The whole roster was playing amazingly well throughout the year. Jason Terry turned out to be a capable combo guard and a second scorer behind Dirk as he averaged above 17 points a night. Josh Howard was able to utilize his athletic gifts and became a good scoring option.

Defensively, Marquis Daniels, Erick Dampier, and shot-blocker extraordinaire DeSagana Diop were all doing their part to deny opponents from scoring. The Dallas Mavericks were a well-oiled machine throughout the season and they were battling it out with the San Antonio Spurs for conference and division supremacy.

Because of his terrific season, Dirk Nowitzki was once again an All-Star. At season's end he was an All-NBA First Team member for the second straight season, averaging 26.6 points, 9 rebounds, and 2.8 assists. Dirk's overall shooting percentages increased as he shot 48% from the field, 40.6% from the three, and 90.1% from the foul line. He powered his team to a 60-22 win-loss record but could not get the first seed and had to settle for fourth. Dirk Nowitzki was also third in the MVP voting, as his good buddy Steve Nash won the award for the second straight season for helping the Suns get to a high playoff berth despite injuries to other key All-Star players. Young sensation LeBron James finished second.

In the first round of the playoffs, Nowitzki faced a fellow international sensation, power forward Pau Gasol. Gasol, a seven-foot Spanish player, was one of the best post scorers in the NBA and was leading a struggling Memphis Grizzlies team to a strong playoff appearance. Sadly, on Pau's part, his team just could not contend with the Mavericks and they were swept easily in the first round. Dirk made easy pickings of his matchup as he outplayed Gasol in the four-game sweep with an average of 31 points in that series.

The Mavs' next playoff opponents were the top-seeded San Antonio Spurs, led by Dirk's eternal rival, Tim Duncan. After a terrific first round, Nowitzki struggled in Game 1 of the Western Semis. He only had 20 points on 8 out of 20 shooting while Duncan outplayed him for 31 points as the Spurs just barely edged out the Mavs by 2 points in Game 1.

Dallas would take revenge against their tormentors in Game 2 to steal a home game. Dirk had 21 points and 9 rebounds to help his team to a blowout 22-point win. In a close Game 3 played in Dallas, the Mavs got away by just one point with a 104-103 win as they took the series lead over the Spurs. Dirk had 27 points in that game. They next took a commanding 3-1 lead in the series as they protected their two home games in an exciting overtime win. Dirk had 28 points in that game as he lived from the free-throw stripe, going 14 out of 15.

Up 3-1 in the series, the Mavs were poised for another run at a possible appearance in the NBA Finals with a berth at the Western Conference Finals. But the Spurs rallied back using their experience and veteran smarts as they outdueled the Mavs in a close Game 5 by merely, stealing that one away by just one point. Duncan beat out Nowitzki with 36 points compared to the latter's 31.

The Mavs next had a chance to close out the series on their home floor. Manu Ginóbili scored 30 off the bench to extend the series to a do-or-die Game 7 and a potential come-from-behind win over the Mavs. Then came an overtime classic in Game 7, in which Nowitzki and Duncan once again duked it out. Dirk had 37 points and 15 boards while Timmy had 41 points and 15 boards. But, in overtime, the Mavs were the better team and ran off to an 8-point win to finally exorcise their Spurs demons and head to the Western Finals.

Dirk and the Mavs once again faced Steve Nash and the Phoenix Suns in a rematch of the previous year's second-round matchup. Though the Suns had the MVP and home court advantage, they were without explosive scoring big man Amar'e Stoudemire and were essentially playing with only role players throughout the whole season. Phoenix took Game 1 on their home floor on the strength of Boris Diaw's 34 points. It was a good game for Dirk, who had 25 points and 19 rebounds. Yet the Suns edged them out by three points. In Game 2, the Mavs protected home court by winning it with a 7-point advantage. Dirk had 30 points in that game to go along with 14 boards.

The Mavs next stole one in Phoenix and gained a 2-1 lead in the series with another 7-point victory. In that game, Nowitzki had 28 points and 17 rebounds. However, Dirk had his worst performance of the season with a horrendous 11-point game on 3 out of 13 in Game 4. The Mavs would lose that one by 20. But Nowitzki quickly bounced back in Game 5 with one of his best career performances. He had 50 points that night to go along with 12 rebounds. He shot 14 out of 26 from the field, including 5 from deep, and also shot 17 out of 18 free throws as the Mavs won by 16. The Dallas-based squad capitalized on their chance to eliminate their opponent and they went on to finish the Suns in six games. Nowitzki had 24 points and 10 rebounds that game. With their Western Conference Finals victory, the Dallas Mavericks and Dirk Nowitzki were heading to their first NBA Finals.

Their opponents in the 2006 NBA Finals were not pushovers. The Miami Heat had enjoyed a fairytale season, beating very good teams like the Bulls, Nets, and the Pistons, who had the best record in the league that season. Plus, the Heat had championship experience as their dominant center, Shaquille O'Neal, had been to the Finals with five teams and won three of those. And if Shaq was not already a huge problem, the Mavs had to contend with their dynamic third-year guard, Dwyane Wade. From the moment of the opening tip, the Heat gave their all to the Mavs. But Dallas rallied to their home crowd on a strong second quarter that they carried over to the fourth to win Game 1. Dirk had a so-so night with only 16 points, but 32 points from Jason Terry were enough for the win.

The Mavs then jumped out to a big lead in Game 2, and although that lead was cut down a bit in the fourth quarter, they were dominant throughout the game and kept the Heat at bay for a 14-point win and a 2-0 series lead. Dirk Nowitzki had 26 points and 16 rebounds—and found himself with one of the best chances in his life to win an NBA title. The Mavericks would also have a big lead entering the fourth quarter of Game 3 and they were looking poised for their franchise's first NBA championship. However, Dwyane Wade happened.

Dallas had a 13-point lead in the fourth quarter with only 6 minutes remaining. But Wade led the comeback of the decade with 42 points to help the Heat cut the series lead down to 2-1. Come Game 4, Dwyane Wade was once again unstoppable on his way to 36 points. The Mavs could not even score in the fourth quarter to at least cut down the deficit to a manageable number. In that game, Dirk had only 16 points on 2 out of 14 shooting as the Heat tied up the series 2-2 with a 24-point win.

Game 5 was the turning point of the series and the one that many believed was stolen away from the Dallas Mavericks. The game was played tightly and was sent into overtime. The Mavs were up by a solitary point with only about nine seconds remaining. The ball was inbounded to Dwyane Wade, who had 43 points at the end of the game. He caught the ball midair and seemingly landed behind the half-court line. It appeared to many to be a backcourt violation, but no call was made.

Next, adding insult to injury, there was a foul signaled and Wade was sent to shoot two free throws. Yet the video replay showed that no Mavericks player was even close to Wade when the controversial call was made. Lastly, as soon as Wade made the first free throw, Mavs coach Avery Johnson told his players to call a timeout if Wade made the second. Josh Howard thought his coach wanted a timeout and signaled it to the refs. That prevented the Mavs from advancing the ball at half court after Wade made the second free throw and it gave them a good look at the basket. In the end, those calls sealed the Mavs' fate.

With Game 6 being played in Dallas, the Mavericks were positive that they could rebound from the fiasco in Game 5, where Dirk Nowitzki was fined $5,000 when he acted out in frustration and kicked a ball into the stands. Dirk led the Mavs to a strong start to Game 6 but Wade was up to the challenge once again. The Heat rallied back from a weak first quarter to lead the game by a point by the second half. With only seconds left and with the Heat up by three, Jason Terry could not convert a three-point basket to send the game into overtime and the Heat came back from a 0-2 deficit to stun the Dallas Mavericks. Dirk Nowitzki had 29 points in that final game and was limited to about 22 points per game throughout the series. Had he played better, the Mavs could have won their first NBA championship. But Wade, the Finals MVP, and the Heat denied them of history.

At the age of 27, Nowitzki could have won a title at the peak of his physical prowess. However, what became clear was that he was not yet ready to take on the responsibility that comes with leading a team all the way to an NBA championship. He may have been one of the best players in the league at that point in his life but he still needed to do more, and be more, if he wanted to win a title.

The MVP Season, Early Exit

Prior to the 2006-07 season, general manager Don Nelson left the Mavericks organization and went on to coach the Golden State Warriors. That move would become costly for the Dallas Mavericks as you will soon learn. Other than the loss of Nelson, the Mavs made no other big moves and decided to keep the core group of players that sent them to the NBA Finals a few months past.

The Dallas Mavericks started the season winless in the first four games. Many thought that they were still depressed from the devastating NBA Finals loss to the Heat. However, in those four losses, Dirk was still scoring like his usual self, even though his teammates did not perform as well as he did. They were blown out twice in that stretch and the worse one of all was a 31-point loss to the Houston Rockets in their second game of the season. However, the Mavericks suddenly turned on the engines and went on to a 12-game win streak after their 0-4 start. The Mavs were so good in that streak that Dirk did not have to score huge numbers to help his team win games throughout the season, though he would have a season best of 43 points against the Indiana Pacers early in January 2007, followed by a 38-point performance two nights later against the Toronto Raptors. Best

71

of all, he was more consistent and more efficient than the season prior.

The Mavericks went on to win 67 games out of 78 after starting the season 0-4. Dirk Nowitzki was once again an All-Star and was regarded as one of the best players on the planet at that time. He went on to win the Most Valuable Player Award due in large part to how he led the Mavs to the best record in the league and their best season in franchise history. He closely edged out Steve Nash, who could have had three straight MVPs but for that award. Dirk averaged 24.6 points, 8.9 rebounds, and 3.4 assists in his MVP season. His best feature was his efficiency from the field as he shot 50.2% from the floor, 41.6% from the three-point arc, and 90.4% from the foul line for his first and only 50-40-90 season. He was only the fifth player in NBA history to join the 50-40-90 club, and his buddy Nash was the latest to do it a season prior. Nowitzki joined the likes of Larry Bird, Mark Price, and Reggie Miller in that club, and all of those players were considered some of the best shooters in NBA history.

With a historic 67-15 regular-season record that was ranked 6th of all-time in league history, the Mavericks were primed for another NBA Finals run. However, they ran into Don Nelson and his daunting Golden State Warriors in the opening round.

Nelson coached a Warriors team that seemed like they had no plays being called. They were the epitome of a free-flowing offense under Nelson and had beaten the Mavericks thrice in the regular season.

Game 1 started and the Warriors immediately pounced on the hapless Mavs. Dallas could not solve the free offense of the Dubs as they went on to lose by 12. Dirk only had 16 points that night. The Mavs shook off the loss and went on to beat the Warriors by 13 in Game 2 thanks to 23 points from Nowitzki and 28 points from Terry. But the Warriors would once again rely on their explosive offense as Jason Richardson led them to an 18-point win in Game 3. Dirk was limited to 20 that night. Relying on their exceptional point guard, Baron Davis, the Golden State Warriors took a commanding 3-1 lead over the Mavericks.

Having been restrained to only 23 points in Game 4, Dirk Nowitzki exploded for 30 in Game 5 to close the gap to 3-2. He seemed like he was back to the form that made him the league's MVP. But the Dubs quickly dispensed that notion. Relying once again on an offensive game that confused the Mavericks, the Warriors went on to win Game 6 and the series with a 111-to-86 win. Nowitzki was horrible in that game with only 8 points on 2 out of 13 shooting. The Warriors became the first eighth-seeded team in NBA history to beat the first seed in a seven-game series.

That first-round exit shocked the whole world, even more than the Mavs themselves. The Mavericks were an amazing regular season team that had won 67 games, but they could not beat an eighth-seeded Warriors team that had barely even won half of their games. It was the Warriors' free-wheeling offense that made the more systematic style of the Mavs confused the entire series. And because of that, many thought that Dirk was "exposed" during that playoff run in that he was not the rightful MVP.

Nowitzki would later call that first-round exit one of the lowest points in his life because he had failed to do enough to beat the Warriors. He only averaged about 19 points in that series on 38.3% shooting, down from his 24 per game and 50% shooting in the regular season. But the great Bill Russell, in his blog, was quick to defend the Mavs by pointing out that the Warriors, having been previously and very recently coached by Don Nelson, had the Mavericks' number ever since the regular season as they beat them in all three of their games.[xv] Nowitzki received his MVP trophy about two weeks after losing to the Warriors in six games.

Even though he was the MVP of the league that season, the award felt empty because it came without the ultimate prize—an NBA championship. Still, by winning the MVP Award, Dirk Nowitzki had climbed up the ranks of the NBA and became one of the best players in the entire league at that point in his career. But what could have ultimately solidified his name as an all-time great was a title. And it took a while after that 2007 MVP Award for Dirk Nowitzki to make a return trip to the Finals.

Another First-Round Exit

Prior to the 2007-08 season, Kevin Garnett of the Minnesota Timberwolves wanted to be traded elsewhere after several unsuccessful seasons with the Wolves. Cuban tried to acquire Garnett but failed to offer a good package of players and a good deal for the salary cap. Hence, Garnett was traded to Boston instead. The Celtics, who also acquired Ray Allen, went on to build a new generation of their Big Three. And because of their failure to acquire another high-profile superstar, the Mavericks had to stick with the core players who took them to a 67-15 regular-season record the previous year. But the same core players could not give them the same number of wins that they had a year ago.

While Dirk Nowitzki continued to play at a superstar level throughout the season, the Mavericks could not replicate the same historic pace that they had a year before. Though the team stuck with their usual core players, some instances prevented them from being able to have the same kind of success in 2006-07. Nowitzki missed a week due to injury and Terry did not have the same kind of production he had when he was a starter the previous year. Devin Harris, as athletic as he was, could not make a difference as a starting point guard, and the Mavericks were suffering a 3-11 win-loss record against teams with winning records. Aside from the lineup and performance problems the Mavs were facing, the other teams in the West, such as the Lakers and the Hornets, were experiencing rejuvenated seasons thanks to MVP candidates Kobe Bryant and Chris Paul.

Because of the relatively unsuccessful year they were having, the Dallas Mavericks traded Devin Harris and several first-round picks to the New Jersey Nets in exchange for veteran All-Star playmaker Jason Kidd. Kidd could not replicate the same scoring or athletic abilities that Harris had, but he provided solid playmaking and veteran experience to the team. On his part, Nowitzki still enjoyed the same kind of individual success that a player of his caliber should have. While he had a few problems with his consistency in scoring, he had several games wherein he scored above 30 points and his season high was a 37-point game against the Portland Trail Blazers in February of 2008. Dirk also recorded his first-ever career triple-double, scoring 29 points, grabbing 10 rebounds, and dishing out 12 assists against the Bucks on February 6th. The highlight of his regular season was when he scored 34 points against the Nets on March 8th. His performance helped him get past Rolando Blackman as the Mavs' all-time leading scorer with 16,644 career points. Although he had a drop-off in performance, Dirk was still an All-Star for the 7th straight season.

At the end of the season, the Kidd trade helped the Mavs limp to a 51-31 win-loss record—a 16-game drop from the year before. Dirk averaged 23.6 points, 8.6 rebounds, and 3.5 assists. He shot about 48% from the floor and 36% from three-point territory. He was demoted to the All-NBA Second Team after three seasons as a member of the First Team. Still, he was instrumental in helping the Mavericks get a playoff seed in the Western Conference, which was once again very competitive that season, seeing as how all eight playoff teams had 50 or more wins.

Nowitzki and the Mavs went on to face the New Orleans Hornets in the first round. The Dallas Mavericks would struggle throughout the series as none of their guards could contain MVP runner-up Chris Paul. They lost the first two games to the Hornets. Dirk scored 31 and 27 in those losses before scoring 32 in a Game 3 win. They would, however, lose the next two games to bow out of the playoffs early in the first round. Nowitzki had 22 in both of those final games. As a result of the unsuccessful season, Avery Johnson was fired. Rick Carlisle replaced Johnson as the head coach of the Mavericks.

Continued Run as the Best Power Forward in the NBA, Playoff Exits

After three straight seasons on the All-NBA First Team, an MVP award, and successful regular seasons with the Dallas Mavericks, one could simply say that Dirk Nowitzki was the best power forward in the NBA entering the 2008-09 season. At 30 years of age and entering his 11th NBA season, Nowitzki was still in the prime of his career and still had enough gas in the tank to continue playing at a high level for a possible run at an NBA title. The Mavs front office would try to give him the teammates he needed for a chance at the championship.

Dirk Nowitzki continued to be the best scorer in the Mavericks' roster. With a top-notch playmaker like Jason Kidd, Dirk found it a lot easier to pick his spots on the floor for open baskets as his point guard would find him. Carlisle's flex offense also allowed scorers like Dirk to have easy looks at the basket, as it relied more on quick cuts rather than individual pick-and-roll situations. As a result of his new playmaker and his new coach's style, Nowitzki would find an increase in his scoring once again. He opened the season with a 36-point game, though it was in a loss against the Rockets. He would have seven games of more than 30 points in his first 20 games. On December 13, 2008, Dirk scored 46 points in a win against the OKC Thunder. Exactly a month later, he scored 44 in a losing effort against the Denver Nuggets.

Just four nights after his 44-point game, Dirk scored 39 against the Jazz. He would score 44 yet again in a tight win against the Chicago Bulls early in February 2009. Twenty days later, he would have his fourth 40-plus game by scoring 41 against the OKC Thunder, the same team he scored 46 against just two months prior. Dirk's efforts would earn him another All-Star game appearance, his 8th overall.

The Mavs would end the season with a 50-32 win-loss record, which was good enough for sixth place in the West. At the end of the season, Nowitzki averaged 25.9 points, 8.4 rebounds, and 2.4 assists while shooting about 48% from the floor and 36% from the downtown arc. He was also back to his usual place in the All-NBA First Team. It was his fourth overall First Team selection and it further solidified his place as the top power forward in the NBA. Dirk also finished fourth in scoring behind Dwyane Wade, LeBron James, and Kobe Bryant, making him the highest-scoring big man in the game.

The Mavericks would face a familiar foe in the form of the San Antonio Spurs in the first round of the playoffs. Once again, Nowitzki and Duncan faced off in an epic playoff showdown. Dirk would only score 19 points in Game 1, but his efforts were enough to secure an 8-point win for his team as they neutralized home court advantage. The Spurs bounced back with a 21-point blowout in Game 2 and Nowitzki would be limited to 14 in that game. The Mavericks took their revenge by blowing out the Spurs with a 21-point victory of their own in Game 2. Nowitzki scored 20 points in that game. Then they took a commanding 3-1 lead in the series with a win in Game 4 as Dirk needed only 12 points to help his team. In the close-out game in San Antonio, Dirk scored 31 big points to eliminate Tim Duncan and the Spurs in just five games.

Facing the second-seeded Denver Nuggets in the next round proved to be a big task for the equally big German power forward. Dirk tried his best to get a win in Denver, but his 28 points were not enough to steal a win. Nowitzki would yet again have a great game with his 35 points in Game 2, but he still could not stop the offensive attack of the Nuggets, nor could his teammates have the same production as he did. Back in Dallas, the Nuggets stole a single-point win in Game 3 to go up 3-0 in the series. Nowitzki had his third straight great game with 33 points. But sadly, it still was not enough to give the Mavs a win.

Dirk Nowitzki would next battle it out with Carmelo Anthony in Game 4 with both players having big games. Melo had 41 and Dirk had 44, but it was the Mavs that got a slim win. Though Dirk would yet again score crazily in Game 5, the Mavs were eliminated by the hot Denver Nuggets. Nowitzki had 32 that game and he averaged 34.4 points the entire series. Though he was playing like an unstoppable man on a mission, his team did not perform as well as he did individually and they were relegated once again to a disappointing playoff exit.

The Mavericks entered the 2009-10 season with renewed optimism and made several offseason moves. The team renewed Kidd's contract as the veteran playmaker was their best option for the point guard position. After all, the Mavs needed to make sure they had someone who could set Nowitzki up while providing leadership from the backcourt. They also traded for versatile veteran forward Shawn Marion in a trade with the Toronto Raptors. In the process, the Mavs got rid of old veterans Devean George, Antoine Wright, and Jerry Stackhouse while also bolstering their lineup with former All-Stars who were yet to win titles.

The offseason moves gave the Mavs a fresh start, with new faces helping the team get wins against top-tier teams like the Lakers, Rockets, and Spurs. In the process of winning, Dirk Nowitzki was still playing up to the standards of the best-scoring big men in the world. He scored 34 points in an opening-game loss to the Wizards but went on to score 40 three games later in a winning effort against the Utah Jazz. He also had 41 points in a victory against the Spurs in the middle of November. Dirk then scored in double figures in the next 14 games before being limited to just five in a loss against Houston. He would renew the hot streak again to 53 regular-season games of double-figure scoring. In those 53 games, his biggest output was a 40-point game in a win against the Portland Trail Blazers. He followed up that performance with 39 points in Sacramento.

In the process of scoring great yet again in the 2009-10 season, Dirk Nowitzki was once again chosen as an All-Star, his 9th straight appearance. After the break, Josh Howard was traded to the Wizards for former All-Star Caron Butler and two capable role players in Brendan Haywood and DeShawn Stevenson. The trade helped Dirk and the Mavs earn the second seed in the

Western Conference with a 55-win season, their 10th straight 50-plus win season. Nowitzki ended the regular season averaging 25 points, 7.7 rebounds, and 2.7 assists. He also reached the 20,000-point mark in January 2010 and was the first-ever European player to reach that milestone. As such, Dirk Nowitzki solidified his claim as arguably the greatest European in league history at that point, even though his career was still far from over. He was also selected to the All-NBA Second Team.

While the Mavs upset the Spurs in their first-round encounter a season before, they would now turn the tables as the higher-seeded team in another first-round playoff series against their Texas rivals. After winning Game 1 on the strength of Dirk's 36 points, the Spurs beat them in Game 2. Though Dirk had 35 points in Game 3, San Antonio took a 2-1 lead in the series. The Spurs limited Nowitzki to 17 in Game 4 to take a commanding 3-1 lead over the higher-seeded team. The Mavs staved off elimination with a 22-point win in Game 5, where Dirk was limited to 15 points. However, a strong first half by the Spurs was enough to eliminate the Mavs and survive a 33-point game by Nowitzki. After beating the Spurs in an upset series victory a year before, the Spurs got their revenge by beating the second-seeded Dallas Mavericks. It was the third time in four years that the Mavs would lose in the first round.

Winning the NBA Championship

The Mavs immediately renewed Dirk Nowitzki's contract by giving their German franchise player an $80-million, four-year contract. With a lot of space remaining in their salary cap, the Mavs were also good contenders in signing the likes of LeBron James, Dwyane Wade, and Chris Bosh (who was a Dallas native), from free agency. Unfortunately, all three of those players signed with the Miami Heat to form the deadliest trio of stars the NBA had seen in a long time. Nevertheless, the Mavs were still able to sign Tyson Chandler to bolster the defensive and rebounding strength of the frontline.

The offseason moves paid off as the Mavs went on to win 24 out of their first 30 games. Nowitzki was still playing like his usual fantastic self in those wins. He had 42 points against the Detroit Pistons, immediately followed by a 34-point game against the OKC Thunder. However, Dirk was injured late in December and the Mavs went on to lose seven out of their next nine outings. After Dirk returned in the middle of January, the Mavs still suffered a losing streak of six games as Nowitzki was still struggling to get back to form. Despite missing a bunch of games due to injury, Dirk was still selected to play his 10th All-Star game. He would help power the Mavs to a 57-25 record, which was good enough for the third seed in the West. Dirk averaged 23 points, 7 rebounds, and 2.6 assists in the season and he was selected to the All-NBA Second Team.

Facing the Portland Trail Blazers in the first round of the 2011 Playoffs was not easy as Nowitzki was matched up with an equally versatile but younger power forward in LaMarcus Aldridge. The two power forwards battled it out in Game 1 with Aldridge having 27 while Dirk had 28. The Mavs took that one with an 8-point advantage. The Mavs then won Game 2 by 12 as Nowitzki scored 33 against his younger counterpart. Portland would take Game 3 on their home floor with Dirk scoring 25. Then, when the Mavericks were up by 23 in the fourth quarter in Game 4, the Blazers went on an epic run to win the game by 2 points thanks to the rejuvenated game of Brandon Roy. With the series tied at two games apiece, the Mavs seemed to be on the verge of yet another collapse—before Nowitzki took over and gave his team two straight wins to advance to the next round. Dirk scored 25 and 33 in those final two games.

In the way of the Mavericks' chance at a Western Conference Finals appearance were the Los Angeles Lakers, the two-time defending champions. But the Lakers seemed to be an ill-prepared team, particularly on the defensive end as Nowitzki, Jason Terry, and backup guard J. J. Barea ran roughshod over the perplexed Los Angeles squad. Dirk's 28 points in Game 1 were not as much as the 36 of Kobe Bryant, but the Mavs still got the win over the higher-seeded team. Game 2 would continue to show how confused a team the Lakers were as the Mavs went on to take both games in LA, led by the 24 of Nowitzki.

Back in Dallas, the Mavs had a chance to sweep the defending champions by winning both of their home games—and indeed, they did. The Lakers could not guard the outside shooting of the Mavs all while Dirk, midseason acquisition Peja Stojaković, and Terry all torched them from outside the arc. Nowitzki had 32 points, including 4 from beyond the three-point line. The Mavs easily closed the Lakers out in Game 4 with a 36-point win. The Lakers even struggled to guard the quicker Maverick guards, as Terry and Barea combined for 54 points off the bench. After sweeping the Lakers, the Mavericks guaranteed the world new NBA champions and denied everyone from seeing a matchup between Kobe's Lakers and LeBron's Heat.

Averaging 25.3 points and 9.3 rebounds while shooting 57.4% from the floor against the Los Angeles Lakers in those four games, Dirk Nowitzki was incredible in that sweep. No one on the Lakers' roster could stop him, even at nearly 33 years old, an age that was technically past peak physical form by NBA standards. The focus that Nowitzki had that season, as well as the way he had perfected his craft, allowed him to dominate the Lakers and the rest of the other teams in that playoff run.

The Mavericks were set to square off against the ultra-young and super-talented Oklahoma City Thunder, who were being led by perennial scoring champion Kevin Durant and spitfire point guard Russell Westbrook. Dirk would enjoy what was perhaps the best playoff series in his entire career as he used his size, experience, and amazing focus to dominate the young and talented Thunder frontline.

Game 1 started and Nowitzki became virtually unguardable on his way to 48 points. Though his defender, Serge Ibaka, was a talented shot-blocker and a good defender with his long arms and athleticism, Dirk was an enigma on the offensive end as he collected foul after foul on his way to 24 out of 24 made from the free-throw stripe. He also put his patented one-legged turnaround fadeaway jump shot to good use to elude the long arms of Ibaka.

Winning Game 1 was the first step toward another Finals appearance. However, OKC bounced back in Game 2 thanks to the all-around play of their superstars. Dirk had 29 points in that game. Nowitzki only scored 18 in Game 3, but the performance was more than enough to claim victory in Oklahoma City. In another shootout with Kevin Durant, who had 40 points in Game 1, Dirk scored 40 of his own to combat the transcendent scorer's 29 points.

Nowitzki continued to torch the Thunder in Game 4 as he continuously used his patented shot and his ability to draw fouls to lead his team to a seven-point overtime win. Game 5 was just as tight as the previous game, but the Mavericks used their veteran smarts to outplay the younger Thunder in the fourth quarter on their way to a 100-96 win. Nowitzki had 26 points in that game and averaged 32.2 in the entire five-game series.

As the Mavericks headed to another NBA Finals appearance, they realized that they did not need another superstar alongside Dirk, they just needed their lone superstar to play at a transcendent level.

The 2011 NBA Finals was a rematch of the 2006 title series. The Dallas Mavericks were powered by the amazing scoring stretch that their big German superstar was generating. On the other side, the Miami Heat was a lot different from their 2006 counterparts, though the team still had the 2006 Finals MVP,

Dwyane Wade. They were also reinforced by two-time MVP LeBron James, who was regarded as the best player in the world at the time, and Chris Bosh, who was a perennial All-Star and a versatile power forward following in the footsteps of Dirk Nowitzki.

Game 1 of the 2011 NBA Finals was played on the defensive side of the court. Both defenses played to full effect but a third-quarter burst by the Heat ultimately gave Miami the 92-84 win. Dirk was solid in that game with 27 points. The Mavs then took away a home game from the Heat as they beat them in Game 2 thanks to a fourth-quarter rally that featured a 15-point comeback. Dirk scored 24 points in that game to lead the Mavs while Wade had 36.

Game 3 was again played defensively as neither team scored more than 90 points. Banking on Dirk's 34 points, it seemed as if the Mavericks were on their way to another double-digit comeback. But it was a game-winning jump shot by Chris Bosh that sealed the game for the Heat who won that one 88 to 86. Dirk nearly forced an overtime but could not pull off a contested jump shot on the other end of the floor. Defending LeBron was the key in Game 4 as the Mavs' defense limited the superstar to just eight points. The scoring duties were once again put on the shoulders of Wade and he seemed poised for his second Finals MVP as the Heat were up 9 early in the final quarter. But as they always do, the Mavericks rallied from the deficit in a back-and-forth game. With only one point separating the Mavs from the Heat, Dirk hit a driving layup with barely 15 seconds left on the clock to stretch the lead to three. Then Wade cut it down to one point and Terry made two free throws to get it back up to three. The Heat ultimately failed to execute in the waning seconds and the Mavs went on to win another tight, exciting come-from-behind win over Miami.

Game 5 was a different affair as the Mavericks wore down the Heat's defense and were able to execute their usual high-scoring game. After being down by one point in the first quarter, the Mavs won every other quarter to win the game 112 to 103. The fourth quarter was carried by a 15-3 rally started by Jason Terry, who either scored or assisted on 11 points. Dirk Nowitzki scored 29 in that game.

With LeBron taking a lot of heat for his lackluster Finals performance, he went on to make his first four shots in Game 6. But the zone defense of the Mavericks got the Heat offense into disarray as they went on to a 21-to-4 run in barely six minutes. Though the Heat mounted a run of their own, the Mavs still held strong to lead the game by nine entering the last quarter. The Mavericks held onto their lead tenaciously, which was even compounded to as much as 12. The Heat could not summon another rally and the Mavs went on to win the game and the NBA championship for the very first time in franchise history.

For his consistent performance in the series and for averaging 26 points in the six-game NBA Finals, Dirk Nowitzki was awarded the 2011 NBA Finals MVP. It was a fitting award for the man who had played out of his mind throughout the entire playoffs and for the man who journeyed all the way from Würzburg, Germany in order to become one of the best players in the whole world. Dirk Nowitzki averaged 27.7 points and 8.1 rebounds in his championship playoff run.

The championship that Dirk Nowitzki won during the 2011 NBA Finals effectively changed the way the entire world saw the big power forward. For sure, prior to winning the NBA championship, Nowitzki was already one of the greatest players in league history and was certainly going to make it into the Hall of Fame. He was, at that time, the best power forward in the NBA, as former rivals Tim Duncan and Kevin Garnett could no longer play as well with their advanced ages. However, despite the fact that the world had respected Dirk Nowitzki and his craft for many years, it was only when he won that title that he truly changed in the eyes of every basketball fan out there.

Aside from the fact that Nowitzki had one of the greatest playoff runs in recent memory when he won the NBA championship, it was the way he won the title that made people rethink his status as one of the greats in the history of the NBA. The Dallas Mavericks at that time did not have any other true star aside from Dirk. As good as Jason Kidd, Shawn Marion, and Jason Terry were at their prime, time was no longer on their side and they were not as good as they had once been.

Meanwhile, Dirk Nowitzki was an aging superstar at that time as well, but it seemed as if his old bones did not inhibit the remarkable way he played during that playoff run. Not only did he dispatch the defending champions and dominate the young, superstar-laden Oklahoma City Thunder squad but he also stood as the lone star who challenged a Miami Heat team that was chock full of the best stars in the entire league.

Nowitzki became a hero in the eyes of plenty of people, especially because he was up against the biggest villains in the entire NBA. He did not have the global status of a LeBron James or the athleticism that came with the best player in the league, but Dirk made sure to do whatever he had to do to cool down the Heat using his fundamental skills and experience. It turned out that his competitive spirit and meticulous focus during the 2011 NBA Finals were all that he needed to dominate the Heat. On top of that, it also helped that Nowitzki played with a collection of former stars who were hungrier for a title than any other collection of players in the entire NBA. They defended well, hit big shots, and played unselfishly all while they were riding the shoulders of their big German star.

When the dust settled and the Dallas Mavericks won the NBA title, the world had seen the rise of a heroic superstar who felled a collection of villains. And while Nowitzki had already solidified his Hall-of-Fame status before he won the title, it was when he won the 2011 championship in such a spectacular way that he was able to change the way the basketball world saw him. Winning the NBA championship, a feat reserved for only the greatest of players, was what ultimately helped him become an all-time great in the history of the sport. And the best part about it was that Nowitzki was not yet done climbing up the ladder as one of the greatest power forwards and players in the annals of basketball.

Championship Hangover Season, Another First-Round Exit

After the Dallas Mavericks won their first NBA title, the NBA went into a lockout shortly after the 2011 NBA Draft. The lockout caused a stagnation in the NBA as teams and players were not allowed to train or make any franchise-related decisions. When a new collective bargaining agreement was put up, the lockout ended in early December, but teams were only allowed to enter training camp from that time up to the middle of the month. The NBA was also shortened to a compressed 66-game season.

The worst part for the Dallas Mavericks, after the lockout, was that Mark Cuban decided that the team needed a lot of salary space due to the new CBA (Continental Basketball Association). Hence, he allowed key players to leave the team via free agency. Tyson Chandler, the team's best defensive player, signed with the New York Knicks. J. J. Barea went to the Timberwolves and Caron Butler went to the Clippers. Peja Stojaković decided to retire after winning the title. All of those players had been very big for Dallas on their way to the NBA championship as they had all been critical contributors that enabled their star, Dirk Nowitzki, to perform at his very best. The Mavs tried to remedy their losses by acquiring reigning Sixth Man of the Year Lamar Odom and veteran former All-Star Vince Carter. Unfortunately, they could not quite fill in the hole left by those key players.

The Dallas Mavericks did not start the season well. They lost to the Miami Heat and the OKC Thunder in their respective championship and playoff rematches. They then lost three straight games before finally winning their final game of 2011. They went on to win 11 of their next 15 games, but it was evident that they were not the same caliber team that had won the NBA title. Dirk, for his part, was not even the same player that won the Finals MVP Award. The long break might have hurt him as much as the change in personnel as he started the season slowly. He scored more than 30 only once in his first 20 games, and there was even a stretch where he scored less than 20 in 5 straight games. However, he would eventually return to his phenomenal self in the next 20 games.

Nowitzki had his share of season highlights. He became one of only 98 players to play in 1,000 career games in the NBA. He also passed Robert Parish as the 20th player on the list of highest career points scored. Dirk then passed another great power forward, Charles Barkley, in the middle of the season. He also earned his 11th straight All-Star game appearance due to his consistent play as one of the best power forwards in the whole league. In the middle of April 2012, Dirk scored his 24,000th point, becoming one of only 19 players in NBA history at that time to have reached that milestone. His highest-scoring games were both against the Utah Jazz, where he scored 40 points on January 3rd and again on April 16th.

Dirk Nowitzki, in his 14th season in the NBA, averaged 21.6 points, 6.7 rebounds, and 2.2 assists. He was selected as a part of the All-NBA Third Team. Though there was a drop-off in his performance, he was still able to lead the Mavs to a 36-30 season and the 7th seed in the Western Conference. The Dallas Mavericks only seemed to be a shell of their championship selves that year, as they were swept by the much-improved OKC Thunder in the first round of the 2012 Playoffs. In those four games, Dirk scored 25, 31, 17, and 34 points—he was the only bright spot for the eliminated defending champions.

Yes, Dirk was still an All-Star that season. However, the implication of that season of struggle for the Dallas Mavericks was that their big German could no longer sustain the same kind of run he had had when they won the title just a year ago. It seemed as if he had poured all of his heart and soul into that title run. After all, Dirk was already 33 years of age during the 2011-12 season and was not getting any younger. And for seven-footers, playing a lot of seasons tends to put tremendous strain on the joints due to their massive frames. Of course, Nowitzki had also endured a lot of banging and physical play during his earlier years. That was why it was common for the NBA to typically see big men regressing earlier than smaller perimeter players.

For Dirk Nowitzki's part, he could still play at the level of an All-Star and was still one of the best power forwards in the entire NBA. With his range, fading jumper, and his ability to score from the post using fundamental moves, he did not rely solely on his physical attributes. He could still dominate games because of how sound his offensive profile always was. However, even the greatest players tend to fold to Father Time. And for Nowitzki's part, he was beginning to feel the effects of the many different injuries he had suffered in the past and the wear and tear had begun to take its toll.

Retooled Roster, Missing the All-Star Team, Missed Playoffs

The Dallas Mavericks, after failing to defend their NBA title, decided to retool the roster, but still made Dirk Nowitzki the focal point of the team because he was still their franchise player despite his advancing age. The front office allowed Jason Kidd and Jason Terry to leave via free agency. Brendan Haywood's contract was also amnestied to make room for new signings. The Mavs brought in young guards O.J. Mayo and Darren Collison to replace the elder Kidd and Terry. Veteran big men such as Chris Kaman and Elton Brand were also added to the roster to help strengthen the frontcourt.

The bad news, however, was that the Mavs would have to miss the services of their future Hall-of-Famer early on because Dirk opted to have knee surgery. Nowitzki missed the first 27 games with the Mavs and went back to business late in December. The Mavs struggled without their best player and they went on to win only 12 of their first 27 games.

Nowitzki came back in a game against the Spurs and only scored 8 points in 20 minutes of action. The Mavs would get blown out in three of the four games after Dirk's return to the lineup, and the big German would not score in the double digits in those first four games as it was evident he was still not back to full form following his surgery. He finally broke out of his slump by scoring 20 back-to-back in losses against New Orleans and Utah. Nowitzki would then continue to score in double digits in his next 25 games. Yet he would have only three 30-point games in the season; his best game was a 35-point game against the Chicago Bulls.

Because of his slow start and because of how the Mavs struggled throughout the season, Nowitzki was not selected to the All-Star game for the first time since 2001. His 11-year All-Star selection streak was brought to an end because of his slow start and lingering effects of the surgery. But though his season was less than stellar, he did reach the 25,000-point milestone late in the season and became only the 17th player in history to ever score 25,000 career points. Dirk averaged 17.3 points, 6.8 rebounds, and 2.5 assists as a 34-year-old veteran. The Mavs, however, barely won half of their games and hobbled to a 41-41 win-loss record. They failed to make the playoffs, thus ending the Dallas Mavericks' 12-year, playoff-appearance streak.

For the first time in more than a decade, the playoffs did not see Dirk Nowitzki and the Dallas Mavericks. The mighty had fallen fast, as it was only two years ago when Dirk and his Mavs gave the world that memorable and heroic title run. But that was when the German star was still younger and healthier and when Dallas had a collection of hungry veterans who had perfectly complemented Dirk's game. The question at that point in time was whether the Dallas Mavericks still had one more playoff run in them with Dirk Nowitzki as their franchise star.

Back to All-Star Status and Playoff Contention

The Dallas Mavericks once again decided to retool the roster. They let Collison, Kaman, and Brand leave via free agency while O.J. Mayo did not choose to return to the team by opting out of his player option. They replaced those role players with capable guards Jose Calderon and Monta Ellis. They also brought in veteran center Sam Dalembert to act as the defensive anchor in the paint.

The additions that the Dallas Mavericks made seemed encouragingly similar to the players they fielded during their 2011 title run. Calderon and Ellis mimicked the games of that of Kidd and Terry. Meanwhile, Dalembert himself was a veteran center who knew how to anchor a defense and protect the basket with his size and length. Could lightning strike twice? Adding such players might have been a pretty good decision on the part of the front office, but everything still hung on the shoulders of their aging franchise big man.

Nowitzki was entering his 16th NBA season. He was no longer the premier-scoring threat he once was and was no longer the best power forward in the NBA. The league was then filled with capable and stellar power forwards like Blake Griffin, LaMarcus Aldridge, Kevin Love, and Anthony Davis, who were all vying for the title of best power forward in the NBA while old greats like Dirk Nowitzki, Tim Duncan, and Kevin Garnett were now playing well past their prime years. It had become a changing of the guard in the NBA, but the old veterans still used their experience and wisdom to throw down the gauntlet and lead teams that had chances of winning titles against teams led by the younger and fresher legs of the new generation of power forwards.

Despite his age, Dirk Nowitzki was still his dependable old self throughout the season as he was now fully recovered from his surgery and back to full health. In all of his first 20 games, he scored in double digits. He then stretched that double-digit scoring streak to 30 before it was cut in a win against the Wizards. Dirk then scored an amazing 40-point output in a win against the New Orleans Pelicans on January 11, 2014, where he was matched up with the younger and more athletic Anthony Davis. He was already 35 years old at that time. He would then score 38 and 34 back-to-back against the Houston Rockets and the Sacramento Kings. His 38 points against the Rockets also included his 26,000th career point.

Nowitzki continued to climb up the career scoring list as he passed Jerry West, Reggie Miller, Alex English, John Havlicek, and Oscar Robertson on his way to the 10th spot for most career points scored. He also went back to the All-Star game, his 12th overall appearance, while leading the Dallas Mavericks to a 49-33 win-loss record. They would return to the playoffs as the 8th seed just a year after missing it and two years after climbing to the mountaintop as the best basketball team in the entire world.

The Mavs pushed the San Antonio Spurs to the limit during their first-round matchup. While the Mavericks lost Game 1 to the Spurs with Dirk scoring only 11 points, they stole Game 2 on the strength of Ellis' 21 points and Nowitzki's 16. They would next gain the series lead in a win on their home floor in Game 3. Dirk had 18 points that game. The Mavs fell to the Spurs in Game 4, where Dirk Nowitzki had 19 points. They would lose again in Game 5 before tying the series up in Game 6. Dirk had 26 and 22 points in those games. But in Game 7, the Mavs just could not contend against their division archrivals as the Spurs won the game by 23. Nowitzki had 22 points in the losing effort and averaged 19.1 points and 8 rebounds in the seven-game series.

After the 2013-14 season, the Mavs would again make roster changes during the offseason. They got Tyson Chandler back from the New York Knicks by trading away Calderon, Dalembert, and two other role players. They got capable point guard Raymond Felton in return, also as a part of that package. The team was also able to acquire veterans Richard Jefferson and Jameer Nelson along with young, athletic Al-Farouq Aminu, though they would lose Vince Carter. Their best move for the season was signing Dirk Nowitzki to a discounted $25-million, three-year deal and acquiring Chandler Parsons from the Houston Rockets with a $46-million, three-year deal.

With the young talent complementing Dirk and Monta, the Mavericks were back to their usual high-scoring pace in the 2014-15 season. They even scored a big 53-point victory against the 76ers. That was the franchise's highest point differential in a victory. Dirk scored 21 points in that game and would once again start a regular-season streak of double-digit scoring.

Nowitzki also continued to rack up the milestones in the 2014-15 season. He became the highest-scoring foreign-born player in league history by surpassing the great Hakeem "The Dream" Olajuwon, whom he also passed on the list of career points scored. Additionally, Dirk passed Elvin Hayes and Moses Malone on the list while scoring his 27,000th and his 28,000th points in the same season. He became one of only four players to have scored 27,000 points with the same franchise. Though his numbers were less than stellar that season, Dirk was still named as an All-Star, his 13th overall appearance, thanks to his remarkable milestone achievements and his continued ability to lead the Mavs. He also reached the 10,000th rebound mark.

At season's end, Nowitzki averaged 17.3 points and 5.9 rebounds. He played less than 30 minutes that season, which was his lowest since his rookie year. Dirk led a Dallas Mavericks team that went 50-32 in the season to take the seventh seed in the West. Dirk and the Mavs would, however, lose to the Houston Rockets in five games. He averaged 21 points in the 2015 Playoffs and his highest-scoring total was 34 in a Game 3 loss.

The Rebuilding Yet Competitive Mavs

The Mavs lost Tyson Chandler once again to free agency prior to the 2015-16 season. They brought in Zaza Pachulia, who would become a double-double machine for the Mavericks. The team was basically retooled once again as leading scorer Monta Ellis went to the Indiana Pacers while they acquired former All-Star Deron Williams and athletic center JaVale McGee among others.

Dirk remained a consistent player throughout the 2015-16 season, even as his numbers and minutes dropped. His highest-scoring outputs were both 31 points against the Los Angeles Clippers and then the Boston Celtics. Both were wins. Dirk was continuing to make an impact for the Mavs as he shot a game-winning jumper against the Los Angeles Lakers on January 26, 2016. After hitting the jumper, Dirk was caught off-balance towards Kobe Bryant, who was resting the game on the Lakers bench. Kobe gave Dirk a tap on the backside to acknowledge what the big German has done throughout his career. The late great Kobe, who would tragically pass away later in January of 2020, had previously announced his retirement at the end of the season. It would have been the 50th duel between two of the greatest scorers and clutch performers in NBA history, had Kobe actually played in that game. In their prime years, both Dirk and Kobe were considered to have the best turnaround fadeaway jump shots in the NBA. Kobe's playful gesture towards Dirk showed that greatness indeed knows greatness.

Dirk Nowitzki, now in his 18th NBA season, was not selected as a reserve for the 2016 All-Star game, what many believed to be one of the biggest snubs, as Nowitzki was enjoying a very good, nod-worthy season for a 37-year-old veteran. He would not make another regular All-Star appearance in his career, since he was already aging and declining at that point in his life. However, he still had some memorable highlight moments, which included surpassing Shaquille O'Neal on the list of career points scored. He became sixth all-time in that regard and was only behind Kareem Abdul-Jabbar, Karl Malone, Kobe Bryant, and Michael Jordan.

Despite not making the All-Star Game, Dirk Nowitzki came up big during the second half of the season as he was pushing his

Mavs hard to a possible appearance in the playoffs. After the midseason break, he went for 21 straight games of scoring in double digits while averaging more than 20 points during that run. In those 20 games, he had a season-high 40-point output against the Portland Trail Blazers. Incidentally, that was the first 40-point game by a 37-year-old since the 2000-01 season when Karl Malone broke that barrier when he was the same age. Even at this late stage of his career, Dirk was still very much capable of putting up incredible performances such as that one.

At the conclusion of the 2015-16 season, the 37-year old Dirk Nowitzki averaged 18.3 points and 6.5 rebounds. He remained the team's leading scorer even though he was playing with guys who were much younger than he. Meanwhile, the Mavs also made the playoffs with a 42-40 record. But they could not get past the first round as the OKC Thunder easily defeated them in five games. During the playoffs, Dirk Nowitzki passed the great Laker legend Elgin Baylor for 15th on the all-time scoring list in playoff history.

After that season, the Mavericks began to struggle to get back to playoff contention as they were still trying to rebuild while grabbing pieces that they thought could potentially help. During the offseason of 2016, they acquired capable forward Harrison Barnes, who was an integral part of the 2015 title run of the

Golden State Warriors and their 73-9 2015-16 season. With Dirk Nowitzki as old and as battered as he was at that point, it was up to Barnes to carry more of the offensive load for the Dallas Mavericks.

Dirk Nowitzki's body began to show signs of more wear and tear during the 2016-17 season. He missed a lot of games during the early portion of the regular season particularly because he was suffering from an ankle problem. It was only during the latter portion of December 2016 that he returned to the lineup on a full-time basis. But he looked like he was not the same player we were used to seeing when he was a younger man.

At 38 years old, Dirk Nowitzki was not supposed to even be playing anymore, but he continued to play admirably even at an age when most players would struggle to get minutes on the court or even reach double digits. But Dirk continued to be a good offensive option for the Mavericks as he climbed up the leaderboards. In fact, when he scored 25 points on the Los Angeles Lakers in a win on March 7, 2017, Dirk Nowitzki became only the sixth player in the history of the NBA to reach the 30,000-point mark in terms of career-scoring totals. To that effect, he was the only non-American player to reach that mark and the third player in league history to score 30,000 points for a single franchise. The other two are Karl Malone and Kobe Bryant.[xvi]

At the end of the regular season, Dirk Nowitzki had the lowest-scoring average of his career since he broke out and became a rising star during the 1999-2000 season. He ended up averaging 14.2 points while shooting 43.7% from the floor for the Dallas Mavericks. Still, at his age, that was pretty impressive, particularly when you consider how banged up Dirk was at that point in his career. This was all thanks to the patented fadeaway jump shot that he could pull off with minimal effort and without even having to rely much on his athletic abilities. After all, even at an advanced age, Lakers legend Kareem Abdul-Jabbar was able to score well and consistently because he had one single go-to move that was practically unguardable. For Kareem, it was the skyhook. For Dirk Nowitzki, it was that fading jump shot that no one in the league could contest or block.

The Dallas Mavericks won only 33 games that year and were not even close to playoff contention. In an attempt to help his team to get back to the hunt for a playoff spot, Dirk Nowitzki opted out of his player option entering the 2017 offseason so that the Dallas Mavericks would have enough cap space to sign capable free agents. His unselfishness was the ultimate sign of loyalty for a man who was always regarded as one of the most selfless players in the entire NBA.[xvii]

Not willing to sign with any other team, Dirk Nowitzki did indeed re-sign with the Dallas Mavericks and took a massive pay cut that allowed the franchise to have more flexibility when it came to their cap space. Nowitzki was no longer about the money (if he had ever been) and was simply playing for the Mavs because he loved the game, loved his team, and because he wanted to help usher in a new crop of youngsters that could possibly push them back to playoff contention. One such player they thought could help them succeed was an amazingly athletic rookie named Dennis Smith Jr., who actually played very well for the Mavs during his first year in the league.

Because the Mavericks had younger and fresher pieces, Dirk was no longer an integral part of the offense but was still an impressive scorer at his age. In fact, he was consistently scoring in double digits, despite the fact that he rarely crossed the 20-point barrier that season. With his limited playing time due to the fact that he could no longer sustain the minutes played by regular starters, Nowitzki made the most out of his touches and was aggressive with his shots every time he touched the ball.

In his 20th season with the Dallas Mavericks, Dirk tied with Kobe Bryant in terms of the greatest number of seasons played with a single franchise. He averaged 12 points in just 25 minutes of action that season and was not able to play out the remaining games of the season because he needed to have his ankle fixed once again. Meanwhile, the Dallas Mavericks struggled and were limited to only 24 wins, the second-lowest they have ever had in the Dirk Nowitzki era.

Despite how poorly the Mavericks played that season, Dirk Nowitzki continued to rise in the record books as an all-time great player. He became only the sixth player in the history of the NBA to log a total of 50,000 career minutes. Most impressively, he did all that with just the Dallas Mavericks at a time when single-team longevity was rare. He also went on to reach 31,000 points that season and moved past Kevin Garnett in total career games played in the NBA.

As poorly as the Dallas Mavericks played all year long, the bad season they had ultimately became a blessing in disguise because they were in position for a high lottery draft pick in what was regarded as a deep and talented 2018 rookie crop that boasted players who could possibly turn a franchise around in an instant. This allowed them to fast-track their rebuilding process as Dirk Nowitzki was more than ready to place the franchise in the capable hands of one of the greatest young superstars the league had seen in a long while.

Final Year in the NBA

During the 2018 offseason, the Dallas Mavericks won the fifth pick of a promising 2018 NBA Draft Class. Throughout the weeks leading up to the draft, the Mavs had their sights set on one particularly interesting talent whom they believed could reinvigorate their ailing franchise. That young man was the 19-year old Slovenian sensation, Luka Dončić.

Dončić, prior to trying his hand at the NBA, was already a professional basketball player at the tender age of 16. He was the youngest player to ever play for Real Madrid back in Europe. And during the 2017-18 season in Europe, Dončić went on to win the Liga ACB MVP, the youngest EuroLeague MVP, and the EuroLeague Final Four MVP, all while playing against grown men after just barely turning 19. As a teenager, Luka Dončić was used to playing against some of the best talents that Europe had to offer—and he was dominating them at times, as evidenced by his MVP win in two of the toughest leagues in all of Europe. He did that by simply relying on fundamental skills that a 6'7" forward would not even be expected to have at such a young age.

Leading up to the draft, while Dončić was indeed a lottery pick thanks to his experience and individual accolades back in Europe, not many NBA teams thought that he was going to carry on what he was able to do with Real Madrid to America. Similar to what scouts thought of Dirk Nowitzki in 1998, Luka Dončić seemed slower and less athletic than the other prospects of the 2018 NBA Draft. That was why he was not considered the consensus top pick. Indeed, the Phoenix Suns ended up drafting the seven-footer Deandre Ayton with their top overall pick. Meanwhile, the Sacramento Kings went with Duke big man Marvin Bagley with the second pick.

Rick Carlisle and the rest of the Dallas Mavericks' front office had been eyeing Dončić and were in agreement that he was the best player for them to draft with their fifth overall pick. However, it became apparent that they were not going to be able to draft Dončić because, according to Carlisle, he was just too good to fall fifth overall that season. Believing that Dončić was going to be a foundational piece for them heading into the future, the Mavericks made a move to have the Atlanta Hawks draft him with the third overall pick and trade him with fifth overall pick Trae Young and a future first-round draft pick.[xviii] This allowed the Dallas Mavericks to secure the services of the player they believed was going to be the face of the franchise after Dirk Nowitzki.

Twenty years since the day they took a gamble and drafted a skinny 20-year-old, seven-foot German named Dirk Nowitzki because they believed his uncanny set of skills would turn him into an all-time great, the Dallas Mavericks took another gamble and selected an "unathletic and slow" 6'7" Slovenian player named Luka Dončić because of his mastery of the fundamental skills of basketball. History repeated itself in a span of 20 years as the Mavericks had now found a suitable European youngster to carry over Dirk Nowitzki's legacy in Dallas.

Nowitzki was entering his 21st season in the league and had broken the record for the most seasons played for a single franchise. Funny enough, Dirk was drafted in 1998, while Luka Dončić was born in February of 1999. That meant that the 40-year-old veteran had been playing in the NBA longer than Luka Dončić had even been on the planet. Dirk, who was not only a father figure in terms of his age, became a mentor to the young Mavericks player.

As a 21-year veteran, Dirk Nowitzki became one of the only two active players who were drafted during the 1990s. The other player was his former teammate, Vince Carter, who was also drafted into the NBA back in 1998. Carter ended up playing until 2020 and retired after a record-breaking 22-year career in the league. As such, Dirk was officially the old man in the league alongside his former teammate.

At first, because of his experience, knowledge, and stature, Dirk Nowitzki was playing the role of mentor to the young sensation, Luka Dončić. However, Dirk realized along the way that the skilled Dončić did not need a lot of mentoring from him because the young Slovenian was playing in a way that belied his age and NBA experience.[xix] Dirk Nowitzki would say time and time again that his young teammate was playing like a ten-year veteran thanks to how high his skill level and basketball IQ already were at that early point in his career.

As the season began, Nowitzki had to miss the first 26 games of the season while recovering from another ankle surgery. Throughout that time, it was Luka Dončić who carried the team on his back as the Mavericks went on to begin the transition from the Nowitzki era to the Dončić rebuilding phase. In fact, Dončić was so good as a rookie that season that the 40-year-old German often joked about how it was the Slovenian who actually took *him* under his wing, instead of him acting as the mentor. Having Dirk teaching Luka the ins and outs of what it was to be a Maverick and play in the NBA made it easier for

Dallas to hand the reins over to Dončić. The Mavericks' trust both in Luka as well as Dirk's beneficent stewardship was so high that they were able to easily trade last year's rookie sensation, Dennis Smith Jr., and their former top scorer, Harrison Barnes.

As for Dirk, it took time for him to score in double digits for the first time that season, as it was not until December 28th that he scored 11 over the New Orleans Pelicans in a loss. The next time he scored in double digits was on January 30, 2019, in a win over the New York Knicks. At that age, he was no longer capable of doing a lot on the floor and had already been slowed down by time and the combination of different injuries he had endured over the course of his NBA career.

Despite the fact that Dirk Nowitzki was silent about when and how he wanted to retire from the game, the world realized just by looking at the way he played that he was ready to move on from the game of basketball and was likely in the final year of his NBA career. That was why the 2018-19 season became a farewell tour of sorts for Nowitzki, who was welcomed warmly by fans around the country wherever the Dallas Mavericks went.

The NBA also made it a point to make that season interesting by marketing Dwyane Wade's farewell tour alongside Dirk

Nowitzki's. While Dirk was the older and more experienced player, he and Wade had some interesting and memorable moments involving one another throughout their careers.

Now, Dirk Nowitzki has had some notable rivalries during his NBA career, including the likes of Tim Duncan and Kevin Garnett, as he fought for power-forward supremacy against those all-time great players during their respective primes. However, when it came down to what it truly meant to be a rival in every sense of the word, Dwyane Wade was arguably the closest one that Dirk Nowitzki has had in his career.

Dirk and D-Wade did not cross paths until they met during the 2006 NBA Finals, where the Dallas Mavericks and the Miami Heat battled for their franchise's first-ever NBA title. Even though Dirk Nowitzki and the Mavericks took Games 1 and 2, the Heat went on to win the next four games and the 2006 NBA Championship on the strength of Dwyane Wade's phenomenal performances. Since then, their rivalry was set in motion between the two superstars because of the circumstances that surrounded the Miami Heat's wins during that series. The loss might have affected Dirk but it only made him a more focused and competitive superstar from then on.

It was when the Mavericks and the Heat once again met during the 2011 NBA Finals when the rivalry intensified and became personal for Nowitzki. While he was never really friends with Dwyane Wade, he began to look at the Heat superstar in a different way during the 2011 NBA Finals, which the Mavericks ultimately won.

Back in 2011, Dwyane Wade had formed a "super team" together with LeBron James and Chris Bosh. His confidence level was at an all-time high, especially considering that the Heat were the clear favorites in that matchup with the Mavs. When Dirk was ill and had to fight through a 101-degree fever in Game 4 while still tying the series up 2-2, Wade and James came into Game 5 seemingly mocking the German superstar by coughing. Dirk Nowitzki saw the act as a childish insult,[xx] and their behavior made the series and the rivalry personal for him.

As we already know, Dirk Nowitzki dominated the Miami Heat in Games 5 and 6 of the 2011 NBA Finals and won his first championship ring. He was so good in that series that even the Miami Heat's president, Pat Riley, said that Nowitzki was the best player in the world in that series. In a way, Dirk was able to get back at D-Wade for that 2006 Finals loss and for that insulting gesture he and LeBron James made heading into Game 5.

117

The rivalry between Dirk Nowitzki and Dwyane Wade never really reached a greater height after the 2011 NBA Finals but everyone knew that they were never casual or particularly friendly with one another. But during the 2018-19 NBA season when they were already in the final legs of their career, they put aside their small rivalry in an attempt to show respect for each other and what they were both able to do for the basketball world. On February 13, 2019, the Dallas Mavericks welcomed the Miami Heat. After the Heat defeated the Mavs in that game, Nowitzki and Wade were seen exchanging their jerseys as they set their differences aside.

Meanwhile, the NBA also showed its respect to Dirk Nowitzki and Dwyane Wade. Even though the two former superstars and all-time greats were far from playing at stellar levels that season, NBA commissioner Adam Silver gave both of them All-Star slots. As such, Dirk Nowitzki became an All-Star for the 14th and final time in his career.

Even though Nowitzki never previously mentioned retiring from the game during the regular season, it was on April 9, 2020, in their final home game, that he made his intentions clear. In that win over the Phoenix Suns, he played like his old self and went on to score 30 points. After the game, he made the announcement to the home crowd that he was officially retiring

118

at the end of the 2018-19 season. To that end, legendary players Charles Barkley, Shawn Kemp, Larry Bird, Scottie Pippen, and Detlef Schrempf all came up to the court to congratulate the all-time great big man for a career that was worthy of the Hall of Fame.

Dirk Nowitzki played his final NBA game on April 10th against the San Antonio Spurs in a loss. He finished that game with a 20-10 double-double, the first and only time he had a double-double that season. Dirk ended the 2018-19 season with career-lows of 7.3 points and 3.1 rebounds. Nevertheless, he was at peace with himself when he left the game in capable hands.

Throughout what was a losing yet hopeful season for the Dallas Mavericks, Slovenian star Luka Dončić made it known to the world that he was taking over for Dirk Nowitzki as the franchise's new superstar and cornerstone for the future. He made it easy for Mavericks fans to move on from the Nowitzki era and support an entirely new dawn in Dallas.

At the same time, the Mavericks also made a trade to acquire All-Star big man Kristaps Porziņģis in an attempt to bolster the team's youth. The Latvian Porziņģis, at 7'3" and with the skills of a guard, was widely regarded as the next version of Dirk Nowitzki due to how he was able to shoot well from the outside and make fundamental plays despite his freakish size at the big man slot. That was why Dirk was able to retire peacefully, as he could simply leave the franchise to the capable hands of Dončić and Porziņģis, and it is also worthy to note that these up-and-comers were both European players who were able to get to the NBA thanks to the bridges that Nowitzki himself helped build.

Retiring after playing 21 seasons in the NBA, Dirk Nowitzki compiled 31,560 career points and 11,489 career rebounds. He retired as the Mavericks' all-time franchise leader in almost all of the stats that mattered. As such, there is no question that the man who gave the Dallas Mavericks their first championship ring is by far the greatest player in the history of the franchise. He is also without a doubt the greatest European player in NBA history and is right up there with the likes of Hakeem Olajuwon for the title of greatest non-American player in the annals of the league.

Chapter 4: International Career

Dirk Nowitzki had been a part of the German national basketball team ever since 1997 when he was still a teenager. His first tournament was the FIBA Euro Championships in 1999. He was the best player and the top scorer for Germany, but the team failed to earn a spot for the Olympic Games in 2000. He then became the highest scorer and the highest rebounder in the 2001 FIBA Euro Championships but failed to get a medal once again as the Germans were bested by Turkey and Spain in both of Germany's medal games. He averaged 28.7 points and 9.1 rebounds in that tournament.

A year later, Dirk led Germany to a strong performance in the 2002 FIBA World Championships. He earned a bronze medal for his home country after winning against New Zealand. They almost made the gold medal game and would have if it were not for a fourth-quarter meltdown against Argentina. Nevertheless, Nowitzki was the tournament MVP that year as he averaged 24 points per game.

The Germans would yet again fail to make the Olympics after a sorry 2003 FIBA Euro Championship tournament, where Nowitzki was playing injured. He still averaged 22.5 points that year with Germany. But in 2005, Dirk came back strong to the same tournament as he led the Germans to a gold medal game. His team would lose in the finals against the Greeks, but Dirk was once again the MVP with averages of 26.7 points (highest that year), and 10.8 rebounds (second highest). Germany would later finish in the top eight of the FIBA World Championships in 2006.

Though the Germans again failed to initially make the 2008 Olympics by finishing only fifth in the European tournament, Dirk Nowitzki led Germany to a qualifying spot by beating Puerto Rico for the final spot in the 2008 Olympic Qualifying Tournament. The 2008 Olympic Games were the first Olympics for the German basketball team since 1992.

Dirk's next appearance for the German team was in the 2011 EuroBasket. Germany finished 9th in that tournament. His next tournament was in 2015, where Germany only won a solitary game. In his international career with the German national basketball team, Dirk Nowitzki averaged 21.5 points and 7.1 rebounds.

Chapter 5: Personal Life

Dirk Nowitzki's family has a strong athletic background. His father, Jörg-Werner, was a world-class handball player. Dirk's mother, Helga, played competitive basketball in her younger years, as did his older sister, Silke.

Silke now works as Dirk's manager and has been working for the NBA TV's international arm. Nowitzki is married to Jessica Olsson. The two met at a charity event in 2010 and dated for two years before tying the knot in 2012 in what was a very low-key ceremony for such a high-profile, global superstar. Olsson is of Kenyan and Swedish descent and worked at a Dallas art gallery.[xxi]

Dirk Nowitzki has also had a life-long, very good relationship with his former mentor, Holger Geschwindner. Hotsch, as Dirk calls him, mentored Dirk in basketball since his teenage years and was responsible for developing his jump shot and passing abilities. He also challenged the seven-foot German to not just become a superstar in Germany, but in the whole world, particularly in the NBA where all the best talents play. Other than teaching Dirk in basketball, he also had his pupil read several books on various topics and had him learn musical instruments because he wanted Dirk to see that there were other things in life aside from basketball, which lasts only up until the body can no longer play.

Dirk also has several close friends in the NBA due to his wacky and uplifting demeanor. His closest friend is probably the two-time MVP Steve Nash, who retired after the 2014-15 season. They grew close as both players were new acquisitions by the Dallas Mavericks in 1998 and both were foreign-born players. Aside from fellow basketball players, Dirk has had a close relationship with team owner Mark Cuban ever since the billionaire took over ownership in 2000. Dirk has loved that Cuban was always there for the organization and was always one of the most active and enthusiastic owners in the league.[xxii]

Dirk founded and runs the Dirk Nowitzki Foundation. The charity group aims to combat the widespread poverty in Africa by providing educational grants and health services to the continent's impoverished children. The foundation has also been providing grants to proposed charity projects since 2009.[xxiii]

Chapter 6: Legacy and Future

When it comes down to it, Dirk Nowitzki is no doubt one of the best players to have ever played, not just in the NBA, but in the whole world. The German seven-footer has enjoyed a long career worthy of the Hall of Fame as he was able to play in the NBA for more than two decades while playing at a high level in all of but a few seasons in those 21 years that he played.

In his career, Nowitzki has averaged 20.7 points, 7.5 rebounds, 2.4 assists, 0.8 steals, and 0.8 blocks. He is a career 47.1% field-goal shooter, a 38% three-point marksman, and an 87.9% free-throw shooter. He has amassed a total of more than 31,500 career points, which is sixth overall in total career points scored in the history of the NBA. He is only behind Kareem Abdul-Jabbar, Karl Malone, LeBron James, Kobe Bryant, and Michael Jordan in that regard. That only proves how dedicated Dirk has been in keeping his body healthy and to how fundamentally sound and consistent he has been throughout his career in the NBA. He is also seventh in NBA history in career free-throws made. Though Dirk was never a rim attacker, he was able to amass almost 7,000 career free-throws because of his jump shot. Defenders closed out on his shot very quickly and he could drive by them to the basket to get fouls.

What also made Dirk Nowitzki such a phenomenal player was his natural size and his work ethic to always improve, game in and game out. He came into the NBA as a raw, seven-foot German 20-year-old who had a shooting touch and passing skills way above any man his size. He worked hard on his game and added a lot of moves to his arsenal. He became a very good player at the low or high posts and developed a lot of pivot moves. Dirk's range at the three-point line also developed as he drew experience in the NBA. He also learned how to blow by opponents for layups and fouls using pump fakes, despite not being the quickest player in his position.

But Nowitzki's deadliest move is definitely the one-legged, fadeaway jump shot. Dirk most often pulled that move off a turnaround post move but used it in any kind of situation. What made this move deadly was that the one-legged fade gave him a lot of separation from his defender while also giving him more vertical lift. Nowitzki then released the ball way up over his head and the move became virtually impossible to guard, even for the best defenders in the NBA.

According to ESPN's *Sports Science*, Dirk had been pulling that shot at such a consistent and difficult angle that it created as much as three feet of space.[xxiv] A lot of NBA players such as Kobe Bryant, Carmelo Anthony, and Kevin Durant have since copied the move that has been affectionately called, "The Dirk." But none of them have been able to replicate it to such an extent that it became their best go-to-move because it takes a lot of balance, skill, and repetition to correctly pull this shot off. The Dirk has often been called the second-most unguardable move in the NBA, just behind Kareem's patented skyhook.

Dirk Nowitzki's fadeaway jumper has also been widely regarded as one of the best fadeaway jump shots in the history of the game. Two other players have fadeaways that are similarly unguardable. Those are Michael Jordan and Kobe Bryant, who mirror each other in a lot of ways and who have fading jump shots that are similar to one another's. As age began to take Jordan's and Bryant's athleticism away during their waning years, they began to shoot more from the midrange and the high-post by relying a lot more on those patented fadeaway jumpers.

In the case of Jordan and Bryant, they used their feet and their ability to fake players with a series of moves to create enough space for them to shoot their fadeaway jumpers. However, the case has always been different for Dirk Nowitzki because of how he mainly took advantage of his height and length while adding more separation with a one-legged hop. As such, it truly is difficult to compare his unique fadeaway jump shot to that of

MJ's and Kobe's. All we know is that their fading jumpers are some of the deadliest moves in the history of the game.

Using his full arsenal of offensive moves, Dirk Nowitzki's career is not without a bevy of achievements. He has been the Eurostar Player of the Year six times in his life while also winning other international awards such as the FIBA World Cup MVP, EuroBasket MVP, and the FIBA Europe Player of the Year. He was also the German Sports Personality of the Year after winning the NBA title in 2011. He has been a 14-time NBA All-Star and has been one of the leaders in that department. Dirk also won the Three-Point Shootout in 2010 and is the tallest winner of that event. He has been a member of the All-NBA team 12 times (four with the First Team, five with the Second Team, and three with the Third Team) and has been the NBA's Most Valuable Player once (2007). Nowitzki's best achievement is the NBA championship he won in the 2011 NBA Finals, wherein he was also the Finals MVP. Not many players have been both league MVP and Finals MVP in their careers. Dirk is one of only an elite few who have achieved that feat.

As a player with the Dallas Mavericks, there is no doubt that Nowitzki is the best player in franchise history. It is not even close or debatable. He has played over 1,500 games in a Mavs uniform and leads in minutes played by over 21,000 minutes ahead of Rolando Blackman. He also leads Blackman in points scored by nearly 15,000 points. Dirk is the franchise leader in total rebounds with over 11,000 career boards. The player behind him only has about 4,500 rebounds with the Mavs. He is also the top free-throw shooter in Mavs history as his made free throws are almost double that of Ronaldo Blackman. And despite not being known for his defense, he is tops in total steals and total rebounds in Mavericks franchise history. Those are only some of the statistical categories that Dirk Nowitzki dominates in Dallas Mavericks franchise records, but that is already enough to convince anyone that he is indeed the best player in their history.

Another legacy that he introduced and ultimately left with the Dallas Mavericks is the legacy of winning. The franchise, prior to Dirk's arrival, was never really a perennial contender. However, the Mavs were able to make the playoffs several times with Dirk Nowitzki as their franchise star. As such, the Dallas fans were able to enjoy about two decades of excellence during the German's time with the team.

And when Dirk Nowitzki left the Dallas Mavericks to retire from the game of basketball for good, he left the team in capable hands to carry on a similar winning tradition. Luka

Dončić and Kristaps Porzingis have both been good enough to begin a new era in Dallas after Nowitzki's retirement. That is why the winning tradition and culture that began with Dirk Nowitzki lives on. Of course, it was Dirk who was responsible for creating an enduring culture of excellence in Dallas.

When ranked among the best players in NBA history, there is also no doubt that Dirk Nowitzki is already the best European player in league history and is up there in terms of international players that have played in the NBA. It may be debatable, as there have been a lot of great international players in the NBA such as Hakeem Olajuwon, Patrick Ewing, Steve Nash, and Tony Parker. But Dirk has scored more points and has played more games than any of those players. Given that, he is easily the best European basketball player in world history as his career achievements and numbers are second to no other European NBA player. Though he might not have accomplished enough to belong amongst the upper echelons of the greatest NBA players of all time, he is certainly in the top 15 and also ranks in the top five best power forwards, together with the likes of Tim Duncan, Karl Malone, Kevin Garnett, and Charles Barkley.

What Dirk has accomplished in his career is nothing short of amazing and has been an inspiration to many basketball players around the world. Dirk was never very athletic. He was never the biggest, nor strongest player in his position. His greatest natural gifts were his seven-foot frame and his unwavering work ethic. He continually worked on his fundamentals, particularly his shooting and his passing, to become one of the best players in league history. He showed everyone that if you keep on improving the fundamental parts of your game and if you keep your body in top shape, you can have a chance at being a top basketball player in any league.

Nowitzki has inspired a whole generation of power forwards and seven-footers to dwell out of the paint and shoot jump shots. Such players include LaMarcus Aldridge, Chris Bosh, Kevin Love, Kristaps Porziņģis, and Blake Griffin. To some extent, good centers like Karl-Anthony Towns and Nikola Vucevic have also emulated Dirk's outside shooting. One thing is for sure, Dirk Nowitzki has been one of the pioneers in turning the NBA into an outside-shooting and floor-spacing league. And, as they say, you are truly one of the greatest players in the NBA if you impacted the league in such a way as to change its complexion. Nowitzki did just that. He is undoubtedly one of the best players the league has had in its long history, and there might never be another player as unique as the seven-foot German.

Final Word/About the Author

I was born and raised in Norwalk, Connecticut. Growing up, I could often be found spending many nights watching basketball, soccer, and football matches with my father in the family living room. I love sports and everything that sports can embody. I believe that sports are one of the most genuine forms of competition, heart, and determination. I write my works to learn more about influential athletes in the hopes that from my writing, you the reader can walk away inspired to put in an equal if not greater amount of hard work and perseverance to pursue your goals. If you enjoyed *Dirk Nowitzki: The Inspiring Story of One of Basketball's Best European Stars,* please leave a review! Also, you can read more of my works on *David Ortiz, Mike Trout, Bryce Harper, Jackie Robinson, Aaron Judge, Odell Beckham Jr., Bill Belichick, Serena Williams, Rafael Nadal, Roger Federer, Novak Djokovic, Richard Sherman, Andrew Luck, Rob Gronkowski, Brett Favre, Calvin Johnson, Drew Brees, J.J. Watt, Colin Kaepernick, Aaron Rodgers, Peyton Manning, Tom Brady, Russell Wilson, Odell Beckham Jr., Bill Belichick, Charles Barkley, Trae Young, Gregg Popovich, Pat Riley, John Wooden, Steve Kerr, Brad Stevens, Red Auerbach, Doc Rivers, Erik Spoelstra, Michael Jordan, LeBron James, Kyrie Irving, Klay Thompson, Stephen Curry,*

Kevin Durant, Russell Westbrook, Anthony Davis, Chris Paul, Blake Griffin, Kobe Bryant, Joakim Noah, Scottie Pippen, Carmelo Anthony, Kevin Love, Grant Hill, Tracy McGrady, Vince Carter, Patrick Ewing, Karl Malone, Tony Parker, Allen Iverson, Hakeem Olajuwon, Reggie Miller, Michael Carter-Williams, John Wall, James Harden, Tim Duncan, Steve Nash, Draymond Green, Kawhi Leonard, Dwyane Wade, Ray Allen, Pau Gasol, Jimmy Butler, Paul Pierce, Manu Ginobili, Pete Maravich, Larry Bird, Kyle Lowry, Jason Kidd, David Robinson, LaMarcus Aldridge, Derrick Rose, Paul George, Kevin Garnett, Chris Paul, Marc Gasol, Yao Ming, Al Horford, Amar'e Stoudemire, DeMar DeRozan, Isaiah Thomas, Kemba Walker, Chris Bosh, Andre Drummond, JJ Redick, DeMarcus Cousins, Wilt Chamberlain, Bradley Beal, Rudy Gobert, Aaron Gordon, Kristaps Porzingis, Nikola Vucevic, Andre Iguodala, Devin Booker, John Stockton, Jeremy Lin, Chris Paul, Pascal Siakam, Jayson Tatum, Gordon Hayward, Nikola Jokic, Bill Russell, Victor Oladipo, Luka Doncic, Ben Simmons, Shaquille O'Neal, Joel Embiid, Donovan Mitchell, Damian Lillard and *Giannis Antetokounmpo* in the Kindle Store. If you love basketball, check out my website at claytongeoffreys.com to join my exclusive list where I let you know about my latest books and give you lots of goodies.

Like what you read? Please leave a review!

I write because I love sharing the stories of influential athletes like Dirk Nowitzki with fantastic readers like you. My readers inspire me to write more so please do not hesitate to let me know what you thought by leaving a review! If you love books on life, basketball, or productivity, check out my website at claytongeoffreys.com to join my exclusive list where I let you know about my latest books. Aside from being the first to hear about my latest releases, you can also download a free copy of *33 Life Lessons: Success Principles, Career Advice & Habits of Successful People*. See you there!

Clayton

References

[i] Henson, Joaquin. "Smooth as Silke". *Philippine Star*. 21 June 2003. Web

[ii] "Sefko: Dad teased Dirk about playing 'woman's' sport' but is proud Mav remained well-grounded". *Sports Day*. 3 October 2010. Web

[iii] Kopf, Peter. "Seven Feet of Würzburg. A seven-foot tall kid from a small German town is living the American Dream". *Atlantic Times*. February 2005. Web

[iv] Kopf, Peter. "Seven Feet of Würzburg. A seven-foot tall kid from a small German town is living the American Dream". *Atlantic Times*. February 2005. Web

[v] Kopf, Peter. "Seven Feet of Würzburg. A seven-foot tall kid from a small German town is living the American Dream". *Atlantic Times*. February 2005. Web

[vi] Gilbert, Cathrin. "'Basketball Is a Dance': Dirk Nowitzki and the Man Who Discovered Him". Spiegel. 9 October 2012. Web

[vii] Gilbert, Cathrin. "'Basketball Is a Dance': Dirk Nowitzki and the Man Who Discovered Him". *Spiegel*. 9 October 2012. Web

[viii] Sauer, Reisner. "Dirk Nowitzki—German Wunderkind". *CoPress Munich*. Pp. 31-34.

[ix] Miron, Jerome. "Dirk Nowitzki would have played college basketball at Kentucky". *USA Today*. 31 March 2014. Web

[x] Sauer, Reisner. "Dirk Nowitzki—German Wunderkind". *CoPress Munich*. Pp. 49-51.

[xi] "Don Nelson on scouting and drafting Dirk Nowitzki, 'The best young player I had ever seen". *Sports Day*. 15 April 2015. Web

[xii] "Dirk Nowitzki". *Notable Biographies*. Web

[xiii] Kopf, Peter. "Seven Feet of Würzburg. A seven-foot tall kid from a small German town is living the American Dream". *Atlantic Times*. February 2005. Web

[xiv] Sauer, Reisner. "Dirk Nowitzki—German Wunderkind". *CoPress Munich*. Pp. 74-75.

[xv] Russell, Bill. "NBA.com Blog: Bill Russell". *NBA.com*. Web

[xvi] "Nowitzki tops 30,000 points, Mavs roll past Lakers, 122-111". *ESPN*. 8 March 2017. Web

[xvii] Winfield, Kristian. "Dirk Nowitzki will reportedly take a massive pay cut to re-sign with Mavericks". *SB Nation*. 6 July 2017. Web

[xviii] Zillgitt, Jeff. "Mavericks believe European sensation Luka Dončić can be a cornerstone like Dirk Nowitzki". *USA Today*. 22 Jun 2018. Web

[xix] Bowe, Josh. "Dirk Nowitzki knows he doesn't have to do much to help

Luka Dončić". *SB Nation* 25 September 2018. Web

[xx] Beck, Howard. "The Ballad of Dirk and Dwyane". *Bleacher Report*. 27 March 2019. Web

[xxi] Koplowitz, Howard. "Dirk Nowitzki Quietly Marries Girlfriend Jessica Olsson". *International Business Times*. 9 August 2012. Web

[xxii] Sierra, Jorge. "Dirk Nowitzki: "Mark Cuban was always there"". *Hoops Hype*. 9 October 2012. Web

[xxiii] *The Dirk Nowitzki Foundation*. Web

[xxiv] Davis, Scott. "How Dirk Nowitzki Invented The Most Unguardable Shot In The NBA". *Business Insider*. 12 November 2014. Web

76328186R00079